THE NATIONAL PARKS COMPROMISED

THE NATIONAL PARKS COMPROMISED:

PORK BARREL POLITICS & AMERICA'S TREASURES

BY

JAMES M. RIDENOUR
DIRECTOR OF THE NATIONAL PARK SERVICE
1989-1993

ICS BOOKS, INC.
MERRILLVILLE, INDIANA

THE NATIONAL PARKS COMPROMISED:
PORK BARREL POLITICS & AMERICA'S TREASURES

Published by:
ICS BOOKS, Inc.
1370 East 86th Place
Merrillville, Indiana 46410
(800) 541-7323

recycled paper

Published in the U.S.A.
All ICS BOOKS titles are printed on 50% recycled paper from pre-consumer waste. All sheets are processed without using acid.

Library of Congress Cataloging-in Publication Data

Ridenour, James M.
    The National Parks Compromised: Pork Barrel Politics and America's
Treasures / James M. Ridenour.
        p.   cm.
    ISBN 1-57034-003-X :
    1. National parks and reserves--Government policy--United States.
I. Title.
E160.R45   1994
353.0086'32'0973--dc20

                                                94-16110
                                                CIP

This book is dedicated to the men and women of the National Park Service. They have the awesome responsibility of preserving this nation's natural and cultural history. They do a fantastic job under trying circumstances. I wish them the best in accomplishing their task and I particularly wish them a wise president and Congress that understand the importance of preserving and protecting the best this nation has to offer.

Introduction

Part One

Part Two

Part Three

Part Four

Part Five

Part Six

Appendix & Index

Foreword

In his book, *The National Parks Compromised*, Jim Ridenour describes a serious dilemma for our country regarding the future of the National Parks System. Jim was Director of the National Park Service during the administration of President George Bush and in that position was responsible for the stewardship of over 80 million acres that make up the 367 units that comprise the National Park System.

The dilemma that Jim continually addressed during his four years as director he appropriately calls the "thinning of the blood" of the national parks. Members of Congress were often more concerned with providing economic benefits for their constituents through the mantel of a national park unit, than preserving and protecting the units already within the system.

As Deputy Secretary of the Interior Department, I encouraged and supported Jim in his efforts to protect our natural resources and to strengthen the National Park System. He was dedicated to the policy that additions to the System must meet the National Park System criteria for inclusion. However, Members of Congress were often more concerned with "bringing home the bacon." To preserve the great natural and cultural heritage of this country for future generations, this "thinning of the blood" must stop.

One might think that being director of the National Park System means a life of luxury trips to inspect our scenic and cultural wonders. In truth, however, the job consists of providing policy, leadership and management for the 367 units, over 80 million acres, in excess of 15,000 employees, and the annual budget of over $1 billion, that make up the national Park Service. Add to this the outside interest groups, general public, concessionaires, and members of Congress and it becomes a rough and tumble challenge that is overlaid with the whims of drifting political winds.

During his tenure, Jim, with the support of President Bush and his administration, nearly doubled the muscle in the National Park Service budget and continually resisted the inclusion of items that would have drained any necessary resources. Jim knew the infrastructure of the parks was and is crumbling, with a current backlog exceeding $2 billion, while millions of dollars are being spent for project that do not meet National Park Service criteria.

As Director, Jim created a new vision for the National Park Service. His top priority was always the protection and preservation of the resource. If there was ever any doubt he erred on the side of protection and preservation. His philosophy was simple, if we don't protect and preserve the resource there will be no resource for future generations.

As Jim continued his efforts to reduce the backlog of the steadily deteriorating infrastructure within the National Park System, he also worked hard to improve the working and living conditions of park employees. Housing for park service employees who are required to live within the Park has badly deteriorated and at many locations is at unacceptable levels. This also is an area that must be adequately funded and money cannot be allowed to be drained away for non-qualifying projects.

During his tenure, Jim developed a new method of dealing with the National Park Service concessionaires. Concessionaires are the individuals and organizations that provide hotels, restaurants, marinas, stores, gift shops and other commercial activity within the parks. This change will make it possible to put millions of tourist dollars directly back into the parks where they are needed, before they are allocated to non-qualifying projects.

Throughout the four years Jim and I served together in the Department of the Interior, I developed a high regard for Jim and his management of the National Park Service. As this book will reveal, it wasn't an easy job, but an extremely important one. He did it well and carried out his stewardship responsibility to the American people.

This book is scattered with humor, emotion and good common sense. It is written by one who was there. I know you will enjoy reading it.

—Frank A. Bracken, Esquire
Deputy Secretary
United States Department of Interior
1989-1993

Acknowledgments

Many contributors helped in pulling this book together. Some may prefer to be recognized. Others might fear retribution and choose to remain anonymous. My thanks go to all those in the National Park Service who checked dates, verified mountain heights, made sure pictures were correctly identified and generally kept me in line. My special thanks goes to park service historians Barry Mackintosh and Ed Bearrs. They are truly marvels of memory.

Special thanks must go to the superintendents and staff at Yellowstone, Yosemite and the Everglades. The Western Regional office at San Francisco was extremely helpful as was the National Capital Region in Washington, D.C.

My thanks to Dean Tony Mobley and Chairman Herbert Brantley of the School of Health, Physical Education and Recreation of Indiana University for encouraging me to find the time to write this book. Also, I want to thank Richard Vaughn of the Indiana University Law Library for helping me to work out the mechanics of putting a book in shape and for his valuable suggestions on content.

The two people I can't thank enough are my wife, Ann, and my long-time colleague and friend Jim Parham. When I typed until the lines blurred together, Ann was there to take over. With her strong sense of what is appropriate in good writing, she saved me from disasters. This she managed to accomplish without causing the loss of the conversational tone I wanted the book to have.

1994 marks our 30th wedding anniversary and Ann edited right to the anniversary day. I appreciate the editing, but more than that, the 30 years.

Sometimes it seems like Jim Parham and I have been colleagues for nearly 30 years but it is actually more like 15. He has served in a number of increasingly responsible positions since we hooked up together in the Indiana Department of Natural Resources in 1981. He served as my executive assistant in Washington and later became assistant director for the NPS. His understanding of the nuances of what went on in the National Park Service during those four years, 1989-1993, was invaluable in my serving this country and in writing this book. He is a dedicated public servant, the kind this country needs, and I wish him the most successful of careers.

Introduction

Thinning the Blood and Blurring the Lines

The National Park Service (NPS) is a large and complex organization. During the time I was director from 1989 to 1993 under the Bush administration, the budget topped $1 billion on an annual basis and we employed between 14 thousand and 19 thousand people depending on the time of year. I had management responsibility for more than 80 million acres—more than four times the size of my home state, Indiana. This acreage along with that under the U.S. Forest Service, the U.S. Fish and Wildlife Service and the Bureau of Land Management composes nearly one third of the entire United States.

More than 280 million visitors come to the national parks each year, and that number is steadily climbing. All the complications of land-use planning, law enforcement, people management and resource protection come along with the job of NPS director. So the job is more than just watching a series of beautiful sunsets—it is a knock-down, drag-out confrontation with myriad interests in how the public lands of this nation are managed.

The NPS is the envy of park officials around the globe. I went to Washington challenged and excited about taking on the top job in the world in my profession and determined to protect the parks that the people of this country had chosen to set aside as the best examples of our nation's cultural and natural history. In studying the work of the early Park Service leaders I became determined to try to live up to their legacy.

The Birth of Our National Park System

Scholars have meticulously researched and recorded the history of the national park movement and the creation of the National Park Service. It is fascinating reading. While I won't replow the same ground, I think there is value in briefly relating the history of the Park Service and its parks to the broader history of this country.

From left to right—jokingly called The Big 4—among them they managed a third of the acres of the United States. Jim Ridenour, Director, NPS; Dale Robertson, chief of the U.S. Forest Service; John Turner, director of the U.S. Fish and Wildlife Service; Cy Jamison, director of the Bureau of Land Management. Taken with a backdrop of glaciers in Glacier Bay, Alaska.

From the beginning of civilization there has been the equivalent of parks—very special natural and cultural places on this earth that cry out for protection, conservation and preservation. It is to the credit of the United States that we recognized this need for protection of critical sites relatively early in our history and began to set them aside for the use, enjoyment and education of succeeding generations.

Recognition of the value and scientific interest of the springs in Hot Springs, Arkansas, led to their reservation by the federal government as early as 1832. It is interesting to note that a country less than sixty years old was already thinking about protecting its "crown jewels."

In 1872 President Ulysses S. Grant signed the act of Congress creating Yellowstone National Park, the first area so named. He had never visited Yellowstone, but the stories, paintings and photographs of those who had made the tough journey there were enough to convince him that it was a place of unique value and should be set aside for scenic and scientific purposes.

Yosemite Valley had been reserved previously, in 1864, by an act of Congress transferring it to California as a state park. The volatile but brilliant John Muir worked to have the surrounding lands made a national park in 1890, and the valley was returned to federal custody as part of Yosemite National Park in 1906.

Two men with different philosophies stand out when discussing the conservation movement of that era. John Muir and Gifford Pinchot spent many years as friends, but the disagreement between them became too great to carry the friendship. Pinchot believed the natural resources of this country were to be used—wisely—for the economic good of the people. He was close to President Teddy Roosevelt and had a great influence on the president's thinking. His leadership of the Forest Service set the standard for the nation's timbering policies for many years. Muir, on the other hand, favored preservation over use. He was much more for leaving nature as he found it and enjoying it for its own sake.

These two philosophies form the heart of the conflict that lives in the Park Service to this day. The conflict is present as well in the Forest Service as it debates the timber-cutting policies of today and tomorrow. How many times have I refereed these arguments of preservation versus use? Much of my public career, dating to my service as director of Indiana's Department of Natural Resources and continuing through my tenure as Park Service director, has been spent in trying to balance the concept of preservation versus use of our great natural and cultural resources.

How can you preserve a resource and still use it? How many people can visit Yosemite Valley before the very features for which the valley was granted park status are ruined? How great is the danger of allowing drilling for geothermal resources next to Yellowstone? Might that drilling tap into the thermals that make Old Faithful faithful? Can you cut trees but save the forest? If you try to make Thomas Edison's home readily accessible to the disabled, have you ruined a piece of history? The question of preservation versus use was on my mind nearly every day of my public life and became an unavoidable part of my private life as well.

No historical account of the Park Service can fail to mention the first NPS director, Stephen T. Mather, and his faithful assistant and successor, Horace M. Albright. These legendary founding fathers of the Park Service succeeded in merging Muir's aesthetic preservation with Pinchot's utilitarian conservation by emphasizing how parks set aside for their scenic value could have substantial economic value as tourism assets.

Mather had established himself as a wealthy young entrepreneur by the early 1900s. He had made his money in a variety of ventures, the most important being the borax industry. Borax is a commodity and, as such, one brand of borax is as good as another, so to make a success of the borax business you must mine it more cheaply, process it more efficiently, or market it more aggressively. It was marketing for which Mather had a flare. He helped coin the 20 Mule Team brand name and make the product a household word. It was this marketing genius that made him an ideal first director of the Park Service.

Albright was much more of a nuts-and-bolts person. If Mather had the genius of promotion, Albright had the tenacity to make sure things got done. Albright, who followed Mather as NPS director in 1929, was a bright young lawyer who was of critical importance in laying the foundation of what became the world's greatest park system. Between the two, and with the support of Secretary of the Interior Franklin K. Lane, they influenced Congress to pass the legislation creating the National Park Service, which President Woodrow Wilson approved in 1916.

Thinning the Blood

In recent and not-so-recent times, members of Congress have blatantly disregarded standards that have been traditionally used in evaluating the creation of new national park units. They have also disregarded the professional opinion of the NPS staff. They have turned "pork barrel" into "park barrel." They are "thinning the blood" of the NPS. Many of the units being voted in by Congress are not worthy of national recognition but get voted in anyway. That thins the quality of the system and puts additional financial demands on an already badly underfunded program. We are not taking care of the Grand Canyons, the Yellowstones, the Everglades and historic sites such as Independence Hall while we spend hundreds of millions of dollars on what can best be described as local or regional economic development sites. To me, that is thinning the blood of the system.

This did not just happen yesterday. There are records going clear back to the early days of the Park Service that illustrate NPS attempts to fight off one park site or another. However, the ball to add new sites to the NPS really got rolling in a big way during the 1970s under the leadership of California Congressman Phil Burton. The House subcommittee dealing with parks authorization was called the Park-of-the-Month Club under Burton's leadership. There are great debates over Burton's motives. Was he trying to get everything under the protection of the NPS with the thought of worrying about paying for it later? Or was he a master park-barrel manipulator? (see *Table of Parks.*)

Good and not-so-good park sites came into the system under Burton's time in the chair, but none that have impacted or will impact the operations of the NPS in a more substantial way than the establishment of the Presidio of San Francisco, a former military base. Burton tagged a few lines onto the law so the Presidio will become a national park site when it is decommissioned as a military base.

The Presidio is truly a great property, but the problem is trying to find the right use of it that will allow for a park-like setting without costing the taxpayers huge sums of money for its operation. I was told that the NPS might expect to spend $40 million a year just for operating expenses. Compare that with the annual operations budget at Yellowstone, which is about $18 million. I hope the planners and politicians can make it work. I especially hope they can make it work without bankrupting the rest of the sites in the NPS.

Another area that came under great scrutiny during my time in office was Steamtown, Congressman Joe McDade's project at Scranton,

Pennsylvania. People were either fiercely for it or fiercely against it. Basically it is a park site made up of a collection of old steam rail engines and a roundhouse that is being turned into a museum. A number of accompanying features includes rides on the trains of an era gone by. It is a charming and expensive project, but it came to be through improper channels, without being approved by the authorizations committee. Projections for completion of the project are in the $60 million range, and no one during my tenure was overly confident that the project wouldn't exceed that estimate.

Should Steamtown be a national park site? I doubt it. Is Steamtown an interesting site that will draw tourists and have a positive impact on the local and regional economy? I think it will. As an economic development project it has great potential, but I don't think it is appropriate as a national park. There are many park sites that fall into the same category.

I could go on describing the misuse of NPS designation, but I'll save that for the body of this book. Suffice it to say that McDade and other members of Congress are not bad people—they are doing exactly what the people who elected them want them to do. Even the projects aren't bad as economic development and tourism projects. But I seriously question whether they are NPS projects.

While I was director I searched for a way to recognize local or regional areas of interest without having to bestow upon them NPS status. Many of the people who would petition us for help weren't sure what they wanted, but they were sure that they wanted some sort of recognition. Often it was the mayor and hardworking members of the community who would come to my office. Some wanted their site to become a NPS site because they no longer could afford to take care of it. Others just wanted a pat on the back and some sign of official acknowledgment that could be put at the city entrance roads.

Without exception, these people were dedicated, well-meaning people, but somehow they had the feeling that the NPS pockets were overflowing with funds, and they only needed a few hundred thousand to get going with their project. They usually didn't know what the annual operating budgets would be for the project in the years ahead.

Over the last two years that I was director, Associate Director Deny Galvin and I searched for some term of recognition that would allow the NPS to formally acknowledge a project, provide some initial start-up help such as providing park planners and some funds, but which would not be designed for the NPS to have a permanent presence in the project. Names like NATIONAL HERITAGE AREA, NATIONAL NATURAL LANDSCAPE, NATIONAL CULTURAL LANDSCAPE, and others were discussed. It is clear that we need some form of recognition that stops short of federal ownership and operation of lands and facilities.

This idea of local interest groups working together with the federal government and others in setting aside and protecting areas in some sort of a partnership is the wave of the future. I strongly urge future administrations and the Congress to seriously tackle this problem before the blood of the NPS becomes so thin that it can no longer support the crown jewels that were and are the treasured backbone of the national park system.

Blurring the Lines

Blurring the lines is a phrase I coined to describe the changing relationship between the various federal land management agencies. The best example I can give is the movement of the U.S. Forest Service toward a stronger outdoor recreation agenda. The episode over the spotted owl didn't start this movement but it sure gave it additional emphasis.

The Forest Service is an agency looking for a mission. Its traditional mission of cutting timber is under attack all across the country. I am not saying the Forest Service will stop all timbering but it will drastically cut back. The cards are stacked against the old timber interest and, to some extent, it is only a matter of time before mining and grazing will be cut back on Forest Service land.

That leaves the Forest Service with a void waiting to be filled and that void will be filled by outdoor recreation enthusiasts, whether they be hikers, bikers, skiers, bird-watchers or others. This change has been coming on for quite a while, so it isn't a surprise to many Forest Service employees. Change doesn't come easily, so we can expect there will be many in-house battles between the forces of the new wave and those trained in more traditional forestry schools.

To some extent the same thing is happening at the Bureau of Land Management (BLM). This bureau manages more than 250 million acres in this country, but some say the bureau gets what is left over after the NPS and the Forest Service have first choice. I don't think that is an accurate analysis, as the BLM has some great pieces of land in key areas of the United States; for example, the great desert areas of Southern California. The BLM is also seeing the handwriting on the wall and is moving toward promoting outdoor recreation.

I see these changes as positive for the NPS. The NPS has always had a leaning toward preservation over use. During my years as director I consistently said that, if push comes to shove, the protection of the resource takes precedence over the public's right to use it. How could I say otherwise? If you use a resource so much that it is destroyed, then the purpose for which the park was established will be gone. I firmly believe that a director of NPS must support preservation over use when crunch time comes.

This move toward outdoor recreation by the other agencies—this blurring of the traditional lines between the agencies—will be good for the NPS. It will encourage the more active outdoor recreation activities to shift off of park lands and onto other federal lands. The fast-growing sport of off-road bicycling can move to less-sensitive areas under the BLM or the Forest Service. If a new campground needs to be built to support Yellowstone or Yosemite, build it on surrounding Forest Service land and provide shuttle service to key park visiting areas. I see the "blurring of the lines" as a win-win situation and healthy for the people and resources of this country.

In the following chapters, I tell of the thrills, the highs, the lows, the pettiness, and also the generosity of those who work for and with the world's greatest park system. I outline the gravest threat to the parks and point a finger toward the halls of Congress. As money is misappropriated on Capitol Hill, our crown jewels are becoming battered and little money may be left to protect and restore them.

Part One

The Human Side of Directing NPS

1

How Do You Get a Job Like That?

The first question most people asked me at the obligatory Washington cocktail parties was, "How do you get a job like director of the National Park Service?" Highly coveted, it is listed in the "top fifty" preferred positions in the entire federal government.

Many think you need little in the way of formal education and experience to qualify. After all, aren't you just going to ride around the country and make sure the parks are clean? People are shocked to discover that administering an agency with more than a billion-dollar budget, 80 million acres of the nation's most treasured national and cultural resources, and fifteen thousand employees is as tough as almost any challenge in private industry. The shock set in for me when I saw the number of lawsuits pending against me in a typical month.

Is the job political? To some extent it is. Do experience and education count? To some extent they do. Does your selection depend on whom you know? To some extent it does. There are no simple answers to these questions. The choice is made by the secretary of the Interior, usually with a healthy dose of advice from the Office of White House Personnel.

This is as it should be. The president by virtue of the elective process has earned the right to control the executive branch of government. Along with that right goes the authority to pick the top leadership in his administration. I would hope that any definition of an administration's top leadership would include the director of the National Park Service.

In my case I had the right education, having obtained both an undergraduate and a graduate degree in recreation and parks management from Indiana University at Bloomington and a master's degree in public administration from the University of Colorado. I was not a total newcomer to the National Park Service. As a teenager I had met and talked with Park Service directors Conrad L. Wirth, George B. Hartzog Jr. and other such people. My great-uncle was Garrett Eppley, a well-known educator in parks and recreation management and chairman of the department at Indiana University from 1947 to 1962. He was on a first-name basis with many Park Service leaders, and conversations around our dinner table with them had a big influence in my life.

Bryant Gumbel, left, and Jim Ridenour
Broadcasting from the shores of the Delaware River, Today was doing a special on the National Parks. While we look pretty happy in this shot, it was pouring cats and dogs and we were drenched.

Almost all my experience was in natural resource management. Before my Park Service appointment I was director of Indiana's Department of

Natural Resources under Governor Bob Orr for eight years. That job, comparable to secretary of the Interior at the state level, included administration of the state parks and duty as state historic preservation officer. I had also been elected chairman of the Great Lakes Commission and the Great Lakes Fisheries Commission, assignments that bolstered my experience in international affairs.

My education was on target, my experience was relevant, and there was just enough political activity in my background to interest the Office of White House Personnel.

As a hobby in the early 1980s, I spent a couple of years helping the Tippecanoe County Indiana Republicans raise funds at the local level. During that time, someone on Dan Quayle's staff wanted to know if I would raise money for Dan's Senate race. Dan was a young congressman from the eastern part of the state while I was located on the west side, near the Illinois border. I agreed to give it a try but warned the staffer that Dan needed recognition more than money from my part of the state. Not many of the west-siders knew much about him and the area was a stronghold of Senator Birch Bayh.

My first fund-raising event for Dan was a five-dollar-per-couple chili supper. How could you lose? Two people could eat for five dollars even if they might have to endure some political speaking. We raised a little money, but because of lousy weather Dan was unable to fly in, so the Republican Senate candidate gained little exposure.

The next event I held was at a local racquetball club where I invited people to try their hand at beating the candidate on the court. I turned out a good crowd, but again the weather was lousy—even worse than before. The party was well under way when I received a call from a Quayle staffer saying that the pilot didn't want to risk the trip. I had begged and pleaded for folks to turn out, and the last thing I wanted was a no-show candidate. I told the staffer they had better give it a try or that was going to be my last fund-raising effort.

When candidate Quayle showed up he looked a little green from the rocky flight. "I'll get even with you, Ridenour," he warned, smiling through clenched teeth. Indeed he did. He plastered me on the racquetball court in front of all my friends, proving to me—as he would to many others—that Dan is a pretty good athlete.

Did Quayle's election to the vice presidency assure me the job of National Park Service director? I doubt it, but I do know he put in a good word for me, as did Senator Richard Lugar, Congressman John Myers, and others of the Hoosier delegation. Actually, I was unaware that I was a serious candidate until I took a trip to Washington on unrelated business and gave the people at White House Personnel a call on the chance I might get to meet someone there face-to-face. I was invited down for a brief chat.

What a madhouse! People were all over the place cramped in tiny cubicles. Résumés were stacked to the ceilings. I was shuffled from office to office with very little privacy and constant interruptions. I got the impression that no one had taken a serious look at my résumé until a minute or two before I showed up. After about an hour of visiting with a number of people I left to catch my plane back to Indiana. I really didn't expect to hear from them again.

About two weeks later I got a call asking if I would be able to come to Washington and meet with Manuel Lujan Jr. the new Interior secretary. These trips were coming out of my own pocket and I gave this some thought before I agreed to come. But my meeting with the secretary went well. He was congenial and had evidently spent time going over my résumé before I arrived. He joked that my credentials qualified me for his job but that he liked his office and wasn't about to leave. It was a pleasant visit but I still had no idea where I stood as I left town.

My wife, Ann, was not anxious to go to Washington. I was ambivalent. Had the interview been for any other position than the Park Service I would gladly have bailed out. As it was, after hearing nothing for another couple of weeks, I called my contact at White House Personnel to tell him I had second thoughts and wanted to take my name out of the hat.

"You can't do that," he said. "We're going to announce your appointment in the next two weeks." What could I say? I didn't know what I would be paid. I didn't know what housing sticker-shock would do to me. I didn't fully grasp just how big the Park Service is. I had little desire to move to Washington, and my wife didn't want to go at all. But this was a once-in-a-lifetime opportunity to fill the highest-ranking job in my profession. Of course I accepted.

2

Meeting the Boss

On April 17, 1989, I was sworn in as the thirteenth director of the National Park Service. Secretary Lujan and his staff arranged a very nice ceremony with all the proper protocol and refreshments.

It didn't take long to find an efficiency apartment, rent some furniture, and start those long, busy and happy days. Looking out the window at night to see the brightly lit Washington Monument and knowing that I was entrusted with its care was pretty heady stuff.

With all that adrenaline flowing, fourteen- to sixteen-hour days were a snap. Ann would not be joining me until her teaching year was over in Indiana, so all I had to do was work. My assistant, Jim Parham, and I settled into a pattern of long days and evenings digging through the mounds of paperwork after the rest of the staff was gone.

My first official audience with President and Mrs. Bush came on Sunday, April 30, 1989, at the two hundredth anniversary of President George Washington's first inauguration. The event was held on the steps of Federal Hall National Memorial in New York City. My deputy director, Herb Cables, and I arrived early to be in the room ahead of the president. When he and Mrs. Bush arrived there was a flurry of excitement as everyone was briefed as to where they would be during the ceremonies. The group in the room was small, and it was obvious that the president wanted to greet each of us.

Over the years I've developed the habit of always introducing myself to busy people no matter how many times we have met in the past. It's a good rule to follow, and over the four years I served President and Mrs. Bush, I always did so.

As Herb and I approached the president I quickly stuck out my hand and said, "Mr. President, I'm Jim Ridenour, your new director of the national parks, and this is Herb Cables, our deputy director." President Bush responded that he was glad to have us on board and looked forward to good things in the parks. He then introduced Herb and me to the first lady. With that famous twinkle in her eye she said, "The National Park Service! You're the guy who takes care of the lawn." I turned to Herb in apparent perplexity and asked, "Do we do that?" He nodded that we did. "And you do it very well," Mrs. Bush assured me.

Ridenour at work in the office. Photo taken 21 June 1991.
Turned to my telephone with my computer close at hand.
This is a typical scene indicating how I spent 10 to 12 hours a
day for four years when in Washington, D.C.

For me this brief encounter started a four-year love affair with this most gracious lady. She was a great admirer of the Park Service and helped us on many occasions. She hosted teas for us at the White House. She was active in our educational programs at the Frederick Douglass National Historic Site in Washington. She served as the honorary chairperson of our seventy-fifth anniversary in 1991. She often commented on the great job the Park Service staff did with the White House and its landscaped grounds. When she did television specials showing off the property she always remarked on our dedicated staff. What a great lift this gave our people! She was proud of us and we were proud of her.

From time to time President Bush would contact me, usually through staff but occasionally in person at some White House function, to talk about one park or another. He obviously enjoyed the out-of-doors. I think that came across to all Americans regardless of political persuasion.

After a trip to the Grand Canyon where he left reporters and staff huffing and puffing to keep up with him on a hike, he dashed off a note to me as he rode back to Washington on Air Force One saying he was proud of our parks and sorry I hadn't been there to enjoy the canyon. I appreciated the note and didn't tell him I wasn't there because some staffer had decided there wasn't room for me on the plane. If the president had known, I guarantee room would have been found.

From left to right—National Capital Region Director Robert Stanton; First Lady Barbara Bush; Jim Ridenour; Gentry Davis, superintendent of National Capital Parks-East; and Carnell Pool, site manager at the Frederick Douglass Memorial Home in Washington, D.C.

The president and his people in the Office of Management and Budget (OMB) were very supportive of what we were trying to do in the

Park Service. Our budgets were always in better shape after OMB scrutiny than they were when they left the Interior Department. Bob Grady at OMB was close to the president and he shared the president's enthusiasm for the out-of-doors. That enthusiasm showed up in our budget and I appreciated it.

As I was chairman of the Committee to Preserve the White House, I spent more time there than one might expect. I was honored by this collateral responsibility, and those long meetings spent in discussing how the White House should be maintained and protected became a favorite activity of mine.

3

Secretary Lujan of New Mexico

The secretary of Interior position has traditionally gone to a westerner. Since Interior has vast holdings in the West, the pressure is always on for the president to pick someone from west of the Mississippi to head up this major branch of government.

President Bush has often been depicted as a man who values loyalty, and loyalty and years of public service is what former Congressman Manuel Lujan had to offer. Being from New Mexico didn't hurt.

I took an instant liking to the secretary. As we sat and chatted by the fireplace in his office, I found him easy to talk to. As the years went on, he would often chide me about being too green—too environmental—and I would remind him that being green was my job. It was his job to hear all points of view from the other bureau directors at Interior, and it was my job and the job of the director of Fish and Wildlife to bring the color green to the negotiating table.

History will look kindly on Manuel Lujan's days as secretary. He was certainly not as flamboyant as James Watt, as lyrical as Stewert Udall, or as tall as Rogers Morton, but he was and is a very bright man with a great touch for the common guy on the street. He hadn't been elected to Congress all those years without the ability to bond with ordinary people in a common-sense way.

He has always been a quick study. I was amazed at the details he could store in his head. I was having to run double time just to try to keep in touch with the park issues. He had my issues to worry about plus the issues of eight other bureaus within Interior. When we would have our weekly staff meetings, the discussions would range from earthquake reports from the U.S. Geological Survey to drilling for oil off the coast of Louisiana from the Division of Oil and Gas; to wetlands protection from the U.S. Fish and Wildlife Service; to Native American issues from the Bureau of Indian Affairs; to protection of the whales in Alaska's Glacier Bay by the NPS. I think he enjoyed the give and take of the sessions with the bureau directors, and he kept in touch with the issues.

If I had to pick a fault of Secretary Lujan, it was his management style. He ran his office like a congressman's office. He spent so many years in constituent services that he was used to having people contact him for one thing or another. As a congressman, he tried to please his constituents. As secretary of Interior, he had a hard time learning that you can't please them all.

He always wanted to respond as quickly as possible when someone would ask him for one thing or another. He was accustomed to turning to a small congressional staff to get a quick answer. Usually the question would have to be researched and answered at the bureau level, and so "Mannygrams" were born. The secretary would grab his pencil and fire off a few scribbled lines to a bureau director and he would set a date by which he wanted an answer. He didn't pass these "Mannygrams" by anyone on his staff—they went directly to the person he thought would have the answer. He knew how to cut red tape.

There were times I was frustrated by the arrival of yet another "Mannygram," but in time I learned to live with them—even to like them. I had to admit I liked to operate in much the same fashion. If I wanted to know what was going on in Yellowstone or the Everglades I usually wanted to talk to the superintendent. That was where I could get the quickest and best answer. It was an efficient way to operate as only two people would be involved in getting the answer—me and the superintendent. If I took the time to go through all the proper channels it would be weeks before I got an answer, and it would be so sanitized by the time I got it that I felt like calling the superintendent just to check to see if I had the right information. Of course, I told the superintendents to let their regional bosses know that I had called so they wouldn't get in trouble with the chain of command.

To give you an idea of Secretary Lujan's common touch I must tell the story of Langston Golf Course and Jack Kent Cooke. Jack Kent Cooke wanted a new stadium for his Washington Redskins of the NFL. The Redskins were always sold out and Cooke wanted more room for luxury skyboxes for the big-hitting entertainment that goes on in Washington. The trouble was that the land Cooke wanted was part of Langston Golf Course, owned by the NPS.

Washington, D.C., is starved for public golf courses. There are lots of fancy private places but only three public courses in the true sense of the word. All of them are on NPS property. Langston has a long and proud history and the neighbors and supporters of Langston weren't interested in losing any ground to Mr. Cooke. The course is in a predominately black area of Washington and many of the nation's best black golfers have teed up at Langston. There is a history of pride in Langston that runs deep in the community.

Secretary Lujan appointed me to negotiate with Mr. Cooke and the city to try to find a way to work out the conflicts. The problem was that Mr. Cooke's operating style was his way or the highway for the Redskins. He wanted what he wanted and if he couldn't have it, he would take his team and go elsewhere. As for what the neighbors at Langston felt, Cooke could go elsewhere, but the mayor of Washington didn't want to see all that downtown revenue leave the city. A long cold war set in.

I decided I should go out to Langston and play a round of golf. I wanted to get a feel for the area and the people. What better way than with my golf clubs on a pretty day? I had participated in a day-long litter cleanup of the river along the fairways at Langston and knew the general lay of the land but hadn't seen it from a golfer's perspective.

I didn't know if Secretary Lujan played golf but I casually mentioned I was going to head out to Langston in the afternoon and wondered if he would like to go along. He said, "They got me so damn busy I can't find time to get lunch, let alone play golf." I let the matter drop.

About half an hour later I got a call. I could tell it was the secretary and he was headed somewhere in his car. "What time are you playing?" he wanted to know. "Around three o'clock," was my answer. "I'll be there," was his reply. Somehow he had snuck away from his staff.

It was already big news that the director of the NPS was coming to play the course at Langston. Now the news was even bigger. The secretary himself was coming. People began to filter into the clubhouse area to see what a secretary of Interior looked like. He arrived at three and jumped out of the car to rummage around in the trunk. He fished out some golf clubs that had the look of the late 1940s about them. He took off his suit coat and loosened his tie. I told him that the pro had arranged for a place for him to change clothes, but he said he wasn't going to change—he was going to roll up the cuffs on his suit pants and he would be ready to go.

Off went the white shirt. With a tee shirt half out of his trousers and his cuffs rolled up and an old hat, he was the perfect picture of a public links hacker. When someone offered him a beer it completed the picture.

As we started for the first tee, someone in the crowd around the clubhouse wanted to know if I was the secretary—I was dressed a little spiffier. I shook my head and pointed in Manuel's direction. I think the guy bonded with the secretary on first sight.

It was decided that the club pro would be the secretary's partner and I found a partner to fill out the foursome. The first hole was over a stretch of backwater from the river. With an appreciative crowd looking on, Manuel proceeded to knock four or five balls into the river. I suggested he start from the other side. He thought that was a good idea. None of us were great—not even the pro—but the secretary was more than just rusty. His swing looked as if it hadn't had an oil change for 150,000 miles. He kept whacking away with an occasional rest and a swig of beer. I don't think Jack Kent Cooke would have fit in at Langston, but the secretary of the United States Department of Interior, Manuel Lujan, could and did. As I said, he has a great common touch.

However, Secretary Lujan was not above putting his foot in his mouth. We all do it occasionally, but when a cabinet-level official does it, it makes news. As a congressman from New Mexico, Secretary Lujan was not accustomed to the press hanging on to his every word. He was quick with a quip and it cost him a few headlines from time to time.

The National Park Foundation was meeting in Mesa Verde National Park and Secretary Lujan had gone to Colorado a day before the meeting to discuss issues relating to tribal water rights and the possibility of a dam being built in southern Colorado. Those that were against the dam were using the often-maligned endangered species argument to head off any construction. One of the reporters questioned Lujan about the possibility that the dam would disturb the habitat of the endangered red squirrel. Secretary Lujan made the remark that he couldn't tell the difference between a red squirrel and a brown one. This statement quickly hit the major press and was the talk of the environmental groups within hours.

The secretary was actually making a pretty good point, as he would later illustrate. He was asking a question that this nation still hasn't answered. Does the endangered species program have the responsibility to protect every subspecies? Does a slight mutation in genes create a new subspecies? Where is the logic to these tough questions?

I arrived in Mesa Verde that night and Mrs. Lujan stopped me as I came in and said, "Manuel lit up the press today." She told me what had happened. The papers had lots of fun with this. I doubt if most of the writers could tell a red squirrel from a brown one but they sure thought the secretary should be able to tell the difference. It was a flip remark, not made in malice, but the squirrel was out of the bag, so to speak. The secretary spent much of his time with the press talking about squirrels over the next few weeks.

About a year later, Secretary Lujan returned to Colorado to attend a symposium on the future of the NPS. It was the highlight event of the seventy-fifth anniversary of the National Park Service. Everyone who was anyone was writing stories about this event and, sure enough, the same reporter was in the small press room I had set up. We scheduled the secretary to meet with the press to discuss the NPS and any other Interior subjects that the press wanted to explore.

Just before Secretary Lujan went into the room I peeked in and noticed that the reporter was seated on the couch. I said to the secretary, "See that guy with the blue tie? He is the reporter who made you famous over the red squirrel comment." The secretary opened the door and went straight to the couch where the reporter was sitting. He sat down and clapped the reporter on the knee and said, "You know, since I last saw you I have learned how to tell the difference between those

35

squirrels!" It was his way of getting the press conference off on a light note and it worked. His press coverage from that meeting was much better than what he had received in Colorado months earlier.

Lujan seemed to know a little about almost any subject. He was intellectually curious and found time to try interesting things. I know he was studying a foreign language in his spare time on airplane trips. I was impressed with the broad character of his knowledge, but one night he gave me a scare. We were at Wolf Trap, the beautiful performing arts center that is a part of NPS responsibility. The profits for the performance that night were to be donated to the NPS to help defray costs associated with the fires in Yellowstone. One of the performers came offstage carrying a very valuable violin. It was a Stradivarius and the performer was cradling it with loving care.

Secretary Lujan asked the performer a number of questions about the violin. My thoughts were on getting the secretary onstage to thank everyone for contributing their dollars to help a great park. I recall doing a double take when I heard the secretary asking if he could play the man's violin. You've got to be kidding me, was my first thought. After watching the secretary play golf, I had a sinking feeling about his holding a violin worth hundreds of thousands of dollars.

The performer looked shaken—but what could he do? In an awkward moment he passed his precious instrument to the secretary, who proceeded to play a credible rendition of "Yankee Doodle."

The Secretary could also be stubborn. He knew that the park concessionaires had a lot of political weight, but he didn't back off of an aggressive program to change the way business was done in the parks. He wanted a better deal for the parks and pressed this issue throughout the entire four years he was secretary. With over six hundred concessions operations to deal with it was rare that a secretary would spend much time looking at an individual contract when it came up for his signature. Not Secretary Lujan. He would get out his pen, paper, and adding machine and put a lot of thought into what was fair for the government and the concessionaire. He never had a hard-and-fast rule but he generally thought that the NPS should be getting 20 percent of the gross revenues of a concessions operation. With some concessions bringing in as much as $85 million a year, getting 20 percent as compared with getting less than 1 percent a year is a big deal.

The secretary would look at all the contracts—big and small. I knew that we couldn't use a "one size fits all" formula for charging a concessionaire. There is a big difference in how a small operator in Yellowstone running a guide service with a string of horses should be compensated compared with a multiservice hotel and food service company running large businesses in many parks. The main point that both sides of the negotiating table had to remember was that the NPS was in the business of protecting the parks. It was my strong feeling that protecting the resource came first. If there was a way to do that and still accommodate large crowds, hotels, and restaurants, fine—but first protect the resource.

Secretary Lujan was testifying on a concessions bill in a heated hearing before Senator Bumpers's Committee on Energy and Natural Resources. Senator Bumpers pointed out that the concessionaire seated directly behind the secretary had called for the secretary's resignation and also said that the secretary was "un-American." This concessionaire was Rex Maughan, a shrewd businessman with a very competitive attitude.

Senator Bumpers wanted to know what the secretary would think of a man who would make a statement like that. Without blinking an eye or turning around to see who was behind him, Secretary Lujan just said, "I would think that the man was misquoted." Lujan's remark drew a big laugh and lowered the temperature of the hearing several degrees.

It would be fair to say that the secretary did not always agree with Park Service interests. Early in the administration there were a number of Reagan holdovers still in administrative positions at Interior, and there was bad blood between the Reagan people and the NPS. Consequently, when official positions of the NPS started up the ladder through the chain of command on the way to the secretary's desk, policy recommendations that we supported would get twisted in strange ways. There were times when I felt that our story was not reaching the secretary.

Our position improved as time went along and the Reagan people left to find other jobs. In the meantime, I worked to establish a personal credibility with the secretary with the objective of having him give me a call when something didn't look quite right. When that would happen, the secretary and I could usually figure out who had muddied the water—and we could search for a rational policy position that would serve the parks and the people without stepping on the toes of other governmental agencies.

In the reverse direction, I would sometimes get orders that the secretary wanted me to do one thing or another. If I had suspicions about the "orders," I felt free to call Secretary Lujan to make sure the orders were coming from him. Often, they were not—they were from someone just using the secretary's name. Name-dropping is big business in government but it doesn't take long to figure out who is doing it and why.

By the end of our four years, I think we converted the secretary to a "parkie." He thoroughly enjoyed visiting the parks and was knowledgeable about our strengths and weaknesses. I knew that he had to balance our interests with the many competing interests that arrived at his door. All we asked was that we get our fair shot to convince him of our position—the same as anyone else.

We got that shot and we did pretty well with it. Scholars and researchers will look at the record years from now. I think they will judge Manuel Lujan a pretty good Secretary of the Interior.

4

Global Friends & Colleagues

The Park Service has a very active division dealing with international activities. It isn't well funded but gets a remarkable amount of work done by partnering with other government agencies to put programs and activities together. Some of my most fascinating experiences at NPS happened while I was involved with people of like mind in other countries who looked to us for cooperation and leadership.

There is a growing awareness of the importance of protecting the great natural and historic areas of the world. While the United States is generally recognized as the first country to develop a national system of parks, other countries have been and are pursuing a strong conservation ethic by setting aside areas of importance to protect.

Many of our international problems and opportunities are with our immediate neighbors, Canada and Mexico. Ecosystems are no great respecters of political boundaries, so activities in one country often have significant consequences in another. It doesn't do us a lot of good to work on environmental problems along the Mexican border unless there is reciprocal activity across the line.

During my four years we were actively involved with Mexico. Each country had its own objectives, and we were able to work toward those objectives in a cooperative spirit. The Park Service was interested in having Mexico join the United States in an effort to protect resources that transcend the border. Mexico shared that interest, and we put words into action by sharing training programs and research. I was told by those briefing me for meetings with Mexican officials that Mexico had laws on the books to protect the environment, but they were woefully weak on enforcement.

I found my Mexican counterpart, Dr. Graciela de la Garza, dedicated to environmental issues and a hard worker. Our meetings would often last late into the evenings, sometimes until ten or eleven o'clock, and I noticed that her staff would remain in the office until they had concluded. I was impressed with their diligence. On the other hand, meetings we jointly scheduled during the day were often delayed or postponed. I attributed this to the location of the meetings in Mexico City, where her office was. I know how hard it is to host a meeting near your workplace. Everyone knows where to find you and interruptions are constant.

I took advantage of one of those postponements to witness one of the most magical sights of my life. I hadn't realized until after we had made our travel plans that we were going to be in Mexico City during the 1991 solar eclipse. We arrived there on July 9 in time to get some rest for the next day's meetings. On the day of the eclipse, Dr. de la Garza was running late and sent her driver to take us to the Pyramids of the Sun and Moon. When we got there I was amazed to see hundreds of thousands of people from all over the world gathering in what turned out to be one of the best places in the world to watch the great event. •

There was a holiday mood with all kinds of bands playing and different religious groups gathered for the activities. People were dancing, singing and chanting. Many of the observers obviously attributed some sort of religious significance to the eclipse. I thought about the movies I saw as a youngster where the hero would say to his captors, "If you don't let me go I will make the sun disappear." I always wondered how they were able to so precisely predict the eclipse in the movies.

As the moment approached I noticed a growing darkness but was not aware that the eclipse was actually occurring until someone handed me special glasses for looking directly at the sun. I was surprised to see it half covered. As the darkness increased, the huge crowd standing shoulder to shoulder on the sides of the Pyramid of the Sun began to shout. The noise level was like that at a Super Bowl as a touchdown is scored. As I watched the chanting crowd, my imagination drifted back to the ancient Mayan culture that had held ceremonies on this very pyramid centuries ago. For a moment I could feel the spirits of the ancient people pulling me back to witness and learn more of their culture. It was a magical feeling I have sometimes felt in visiting some of our own Native American sites such as Mesa Verde. I will never forget it.

In February 1992 I was invited to be a keynote speaker at the Fourth World Conference on National Parks and Protected Areas, held in Caracas, Venezuela. Leaders of parks and protected areas from all over the world would attend, and the NPS was expected and honored to have a leading role at the conference.

A week or so beforehand an unsuccessful coup attempt was made on the life of Carlos Andres Perez, the president of Venezuela. We didn't know if the conference would be postponed, or if we would attend in any event. As I worked on my speech we awaited the go/no-go decision from the State Department. I got the impression that the people over at State didn't want to risk our being put into a possible hostage-type situation but were interested in showing our flag as an indication of our confidence that the government of Venezuela would work out its problems. The word came down that we should go as planned.

I arrived a day early, as I wanted to give at least the first portion of my speech in Spanish and I needed time to practice. I don't speak Spanish but would give the speech phonetically. I wished I had worked harder on Spanish in college.

On the way in from the airport I was surprised to hear the cab driver speak so openly about the failed coup attempt. The military in full battle gear was all over the airport and appeared to be on a high level of alert. This didn't seem to bother the cab driver at all. He voiced his opinion that those who attempted the coup weren't very bright, as they had attacked the president's palace and only succeeded in badly scaring the president's wife. "Everyone knows the president doesn't sleep at the palace; he sleeps in the suburbs with his mistress," he said.

I would get my chance to meet President Perez on the day of my speech, as he was scheduled to welcome us to the country. I was hoping I wouldn't be seated next to him in the event the coup attempt might start up again.

It seemed unwise to be walking the streets when everyone else appeared to have a gun, so I didn't stray far from the hotel. I swam in the pool there and practiced my speech on members of our delegation who spoke Spanish to see if they could understand what I was saying. It wasn't great, but I got better over the next day and was ready to walk to the convention center for the big moment. When I arrived I was told that I should go to a special entrance where the speakers were to gather.

There were soldiers with machine guns everywhere. I hadn't felt the threat of gunfire since my days in Vietnam. But the conference delegates seemed to be in a festive mood and not worried about the machine guns, so why should I be? As I approached the door a number of soldiers barred my way and started speaking to me in very rapid Spanish. I had no idea what they were saying. I kept pointing to my name tag and the door but it did no good. They talked faster and the pitch in their voices got higher. They looked very serious and I was making no progress.

A man in the crowd moving toward the main entrance shouted out to me, "Señor, they want to know if you have a gun." I felt like shouting back, "No, but do I need one?" I later found out that they had collected a number of guns at the door. It seems that many of the delegates from the different countries had brought along bodyguards. I remembered that our own Park Police had asked to accompany me on the trip and I had vetoed the idea with the thought that they were just looking for a few days of fun in the sun. Maybe I should have given that decision more thought!

While in Venezuela I was treated to another great sight. A note was under my door offering me the chance to visit a very rural and rugged area of southern Venezuela that was being studied for its tourist potential. It would be an all-day trip and I was to be prepared for rugged hiking and water adventure in a remote part of the country. It sounded like an Indiana Jones adventure, especially with the smell of the coup attempt in the air, but I couldn't pass it up. Up at 5AM and off to someplace I had never heard of at the invitation of someone I didn't know in a country I had never been to with a language I couldn't speak or understand—I doubted the State Department would have approved.

I started the trip by jet, but after a short leg switched to a small six-passenger prop plane that looked as though it had been around for a while. We were headed to Angel Falls, the world's tallest waterfall at approximately 3,300 feet. Compare this with Niagara's 167 feet and you get an idea of what an awesome sight we saw.

The pilot gave us a close look at the falls while telling the story of an American pilot, Jimmy Angel, who had crashed on the great flat-topped mountain at the top of the falls while attempting to land. These huge flat-topped mountains are spectacular, and the view of the falls took my breath away. The problem, my host had written on a note, was to find a way to bring tourists to this area without destroying the great natural beauty that was the attraction. Of course, we have the very same problem in the United States and have made some progress in dealing with it.

We circled the mountain and alighted by a small village of six to ten huts. We were greeted by a small but powerfully built native wearing a loincloth. He reminded me of Tattoo from the television show "Fantasy Island." He led us to a hut that we could use as a changing area. Our English-speaking guide said the native would be hiking with us and told us to call him Joe. I noticed Joe had a blowgun and hoped it was for show.

Our guide told us to put on something expendable and be sure to have something on our feet to protect us from slipping. I had just bought a new pair of Nikes and was determined not to ruin them on my first trip, so I decided I could wear them and take them off when we got into water.

"Getting into water" doesn't describe the unbelievable waterfalls and streams we saw that day. "Spectacular" doesn't even start to describe it.

The first falls we came to were not terribly high and the water felt great after the hike. Our guide asked if anyone would like to climb the walls of the canyon to get to the top of the falls. It seemed like a good idea at the time. At the top was a somewhat level area where you could walk out on a ledge and get under the falls for a bracing shower, but the guide warned us it was very slick. I wasn't about to ruin my new shoes so I took them off and edged my way onto the ledge. I looked back down to those who had decided not to make the climb and wondered why I wasn't with them.

I almost got my wish as my wet, bare feet betrayed me and I started a slow but sure slide toward the edge. I didn't completely panic, but I sure sat down fast. That slowed but didn't stop my slide, and my fear mounted. Now I was looking for anything possible to grab onto. Suddenly a small but very strong hand grabbed my arm. It was Joe, and that little guy was strong. He pulled me back to safety with a wide grin on his face. I put on my Nikes and didn't take them off again for the entire trip.

The final leg of our journey took us to a small lake we needed to swim across to see the "best waterfall," according to our guide. Joe would bring across those who couldn't swim in a small dugout canoe. Swimming sounded good and the lake wasn't large. Once on the other side we entered a water-filled crevasse in which we would swim part of the way and wade the rest.

The crevasse itself was beautiful. At places it was no wider than a stretch of my arms, and you could look straight up—possibly two hundred feet to the top of the crevasse—to see the blue sky. Little ferns and other plants were growing everywhere and small waterfalls trickled down both sides. As we approached the final bend in the crevasse we could hear the sound of a powerful waterfall. Rounding the bend we saw a solid sheet of water. Joe, who was leading us, walked through the waterfall and disappeared. He was good at appearing and disappearing—it was part of the adventure for me.

Joe reappeared in the waterfall and motioned for us to move ahead. With some doubt as to why I was doing this, I plunged in and, after four or five steps, found myself on the other side in a bowl of spectacular waterfalls. What an unbelievable sight! Even Indiana Jones would have been impressed. We rested and played there for an hour, then started the trip back.

Our trip back on the small plane took us to the charming town of Bolívar where we saw the church wall that had served as the place of many executions over hundreds of years. We watched night fall over the Orinoco River. The day had been long but one I wouldn't have missed.

Back on the jet and headed for Caracas I thought that the Park Service could help Venezuela develop a sustainable tourism plan for visitors to enjoy this magnificent trip. The plan would have to be carefully thought through. The area was too fragile to accept large numbers of visitors. The footpaths were already becoming quite worn, large numbers would overwhelm the local tribes, and the spirit of adventure I had felt would be lost. The trip would also have to be rather expensive with all the airplane trips and the special arrangements. If it were easy and inexpensive the numbers of visitors would grow dramatically and the special quality of the experience would be ruined. I drifted off to sleep pondering the possibilities.

On another trip, this time to England, I found the parks there organized much differently than our traditional parks. The easiest way to explain this difference grew out of a reaction I got from a gathering of England's park employees.

In my remarks I mentioned that the Park Service has the largest public approval rating of any U.S. federal agency. This drew a big laugh from my audience. They said their parks program might get an award for being least popular. I couldn't understand why that would be: the areas I had seen were beautiful. They explained that, for the most part, the government did not own the parks. Instead, it protected the areas with a very heavy dose of zoning intended to keep things as they were. Getting a permit to paint your house a different color or build a new house was extremely difficult. Everyone who has served on a zoning board knows that this is not the most popular thing to do. Every petitioner thinks it is only fair that he or she gets the change requested, and everyone who is against the change is angry if the petitioner gets it.

That's how they keep those quaint English villages quaint. Individual freedoms with private property are limited. I doubt I could sell that concept in Idaho or Alaska, but historic-district ordinances have controlled development for decades in some of our older communities, including Charleston, South Carolina; New Orleans, Louisiana; Alexandria, Virginia; and the Georgetown section of Washington, D.C. Parks in and around such places depend on strong local zoning to maintain their historic environments.

This last anecdote relates to our international park venture with what was then the Soviet Union. This was very close to being a done deal when the shakeup in Russia occurred.

Bering Land Bridge National Preserve, containing nearly 2.8 million acres, is a remnant of the isthmus that connected Alaska with Siberia more than thirteen thousand years ago. NPS Associate Director Deny

Galvin led our efforts to set up a sister park arrangement with the Soviet Union across the Bering Strait. President Bush and USSR President Gorbachev signed off on the concept at their meeting in 1990. President Bush and President Yeltsin reaffirmed the agreement to move ahead at their 1992 meeting. There seemed to be a little foot-dragging on the Russian side, but I was confident we were going to get the job done.

Then one day I was asked to meet a Russian representative who was being briefed in our conference room. We exchanged pleasantries and I listened in on the briefing. What was being said sounded very familiar. I motioned for one of those doing the briefing to join me outside the room.

"Why are we going over all these issues again?" I asked. "This is old stuff we've hashed out many times before." This was a Yeltsin man, I was told, and we were starting over with new management. There were concerns and confusion in Russia over land ownership. The Russians thought there would need to be public hearings and they weren't used to holding them. I had to chuckle. These people are going to learn all about public hearings. The cost of government just went up and the pace just slowed down. Welcome to democracy.

There were many international involvements of the Park Service while I was director. We were helping to restore the Taj Mahal and design a visitor plan that would do a better job of protecting it in the future. We had people working in Latin America and Africa as well as the former Soviet republics.

One Russian gave us a very interesting and humorous slide presentation. As he went through each slide of a beautiful park area he would describe it: "This is so-and-so national park, unfortunately no longer part of the Soviet Union." While he treated the subject with humor, I could hear a trace of sadness in his voice. His world was changing rapidly.

5

Our Dedicated Park Service People

As you may have gathered from the previous chapter, being NPS director is not all work and no play. While enjoying and learning from some of the earth's most spectacular wonders, I was often reminded of the hard work and dedication of our Park Service people.

Typically, I visited NPS sites for a specific purpose such as inspecting land acquisition possibilities or inspecting badly worn infrastructure in need of budget support. However, in the summer of 1990, Ann and I and our son Kyle took a whirlwind trip of some incredible California parks: Yosemite, Sequoia, Golden Gate, Point Reyes National Seashore, Muir Woods, Channel Islands and the Presidio, scheduled to become NPS property. That is a lot of traveling in a short period of time and the superintendents, true to their calling, wanted me to see everything, including all the beauty—and all the things that needed fixing.

At Yosemite, I stayed in the valley while my wife and son went up to visit Inspiration Point. A favorite spot for tourists, Inspiration Point has a magnificent view over the entire valley. I was holding a press conference announcing plans to move some park operations buildings out of the valley to a spot where they wouldn't be so conspicuous. By moving the vehicle-maintenance facilities to the park's edge we could also save some traffic from coming into the heart of the park—the traffic of our own workers.

Ann and Kyle both love to hike and decided they would hike down from Inspiration Point to the valley floor to meet me. The distance is about five miles and it is fairly rugged hiking, but they didn't mind except for a storm that was forming over the park. That storm moved in very quickly and in a matter of an hour or two, there were numerous lightning-strike blazes going on in the park. The park was dry and the fires were hot. I had visions of another Yellowstone situation.

47

From left to right—Associate Director for Operations Jack Morehead; Mike Corbett, climbing partner of Ranger Wellman; Ranger Mark Wellman; President George Bush; Jim Ridenour, director, National Park Service.

Although paralyzed from the waist down from a rock climbing accident, Ranger Mark Wellman captured the attention of the nation by climbing El Capitan in Yosemite National Park. Climbing with Mike Corbett, Wellman made the 7,042-foot climb in nine days. The climb was covered by national network news and caught President Bush's attention. President Bush strongly backed a program of support for those with disabilities and asked if we could bring Ranger Wellman to the White House to discuss issues of accessibility.

Mark was worried that he wouldn't be properly dressed as he didn't own a suit. I assured him that the ranger uniform was perfectly appropriate. When we entered the Oval Office, the president exclaimed, "There is the guy who is getting more prime time coverage that I am getting." We had a very nice 15-minute chat with the president, who was extremely interested in questions of accessibility.

We were due at Sequoia the next day and, if we stayed at Yosemite any longer, we might not get out of the park. They were closing down roads rapidly and we were among the last of the cars to head for the south gate. Before those fires were out, they burned over twenty-five thousand acres including an area named Foresta that contained homes and summer cottages. All in all, seventy structures and fourteen vehicles were lost when the wind shifted and sent that fire into the Foresta area. Later that week when I returned and walked the area of the fires, I was amazed that there were no deaths and that injuries were at a minimum. The NPS firefighters know what they are doing and come prepared. I spent an evening in one of the base camps and shared dinner with hungry and exhausted but happy firefighters. They were doing what they were trained to do and there was a great spirit of camaraderie as groups would gather together to reminisce about fires they had fought in the past.

Another example of the dedication of NPS people came when we faced the massive cleanup of the *Exxon Valdez* oil spill. Trying to rescue the natural and cultural resources along the beaches of the parks was an incredibly difficult task and the weather and working conditions were tough. Yet we had no shortage of NPS personnel who volunteered to leave their posts in other parts of the country to take on this difficult task. Not only did our regular employees come to the rescue: I was amazed and gratified to see how many of our retired employees joined in the clean-up effort.

Volunteers are a big part of the NPS success story. When I came to the Park Service we averaged around thirty thousand volunteers a year. When I left, that number was over seventy-five thousand a year.

Stories of dedication repeated themselves as hurricanes ripped through the Virgin Islands in 1990 and South Florida in 1992. The devastation was beyond belief in both instances but NPS rescue and recovery teams were on their way to the sites almost before the storms had ended.

Ping Crawford, superintendent at San Juan National Historic Site in Puerto Rico, is an excellent pilot. He jumped into his own small plane and was on the way to the Virgin Islands before the air strips had been cleared of all the damaged and wrecked planes. He knew that our people were in a highly stressful and potentially dangerous situation. He did not know what conditions he would find but he did know that NPS people needed help and that they were all part of the family.

Hurricane Hugo brought massive destruction to the Everglades. The natural environment held up much better than the man-made structures in the park, but the biggest problem was that a high percentage of our employees lost their homes and everything they had. We were fortunate to have Ranger Rick Gale, a veteran of many NPS emergencies, lead an emergency management team to the Everglades to begin immediate rescue and rehabilitation for the park and the park families. Conditions in South Florida were difficult. It was hot and muggy. There was no electricity and that meant no air conditioning or refrigeration. We weren't sure of where all our employees were.

Superintendent Dick Ring and Rick and his well-trained staff did the best job of all the rescue teams in South Florida in bringing order out of chaos. T W Services, our park concessionaire, provided emergency rations for our employees and the rescue team. We were saddened but felt fortunate to suffer only one death in that destructive storm.

In the spring of 1990, while I toured the Everglades by helicopter, Ann spent the day with Sandy Dayhoff, Everglades National Park educational specialist and a busload of school children from Miami. Sandy pioneered the Everglades environmental program for inner city Dade County schoolchildren. Children who rarely leave the city excitedly identified alligators and talked knowingly about the alligators' grass nests, each of which contains up to 30 eggs. Ann told me about a fascinating discussion that Sandy held with the schoolchildren about the fact that moisture and heat being necessary to incubate alligator eggs. Sandy asked the children if they thought there might be a connection to the disappearance of dinosaurs. The kids were not only interested but also excited about this discussion.

Sandy had invested years of preparation with the local teachers, and the children were well prepared and anticipating what they would see and hear on the park tour. She identified the big black and white wood ibis, a rigid gray heron, the bold otter. Beyond that, she coached them in the ecological lessons of the Everglades, the wetlands upon which all life in South Florida depends. As Marjory Stoneman Douglas admonishes in her book, *The Everglades: River of Grass, (p.308)*

> The future of South Florida, as for all once-beautiful and despoiled areas of our country, lies in aroused and informed public opinion and citizen action.

After returning to the educational headquarters, Ann located the bathhouse but could not find a sign identifying the girls' room. Sandy expected the children to remember the lessons they had been taught and had placed pictures of a male anhinga over the boys' room and a female anhinga over the girls' room. A close observer on the school bus trip was expected to find the right room. Ann admitted she had to guess.

During a tour of Hawaii, that lush and magnificent paradise, I had the opportunity to see the beauty of *human* nature.

On a side trip to Molokai, I had one of the most touching experiences of my tenure as NPS director. The NPS is gradually taking over the leper colony that is located in an extremely difficult place to reach—either by sea or by land. It is called Kalaupapa National Historic Park and is available for public visitation on a limited basis. You must get permission from the Hawaii Department of Health to visit and your tour arrangements must be made through a tour company owned by the remaining residents of Kalaupapa.

The residents were banished to this beautiful area—not for committing a crime, but for contracting what was commonly called leprosy in those days but is now more properly called Hansen's disease. They were sent here for the health and safety of the general public. Some were sent as small children and have never left this isolated part of the island. With the help of modern medicine, these people are no longer a threat to the general population but many of them have spent fifty or sixty years on the island and say they have no reason to want to leave.

One fellow told me of his arrival to Kalaupapa after being banished from one of the other islands in the Hawaiian chain. He said that the seas were rough and treacherous—and the ship captain did not want to risk his boat by getting too close to shore. As the captain neared the rocky shore, the young boy, who was six or seven years old at the time, was thrown overboard with nothing but a small sack of provisions slung around his neck. There was little reason to believe the boy would ever make it to shore alive. He did make it and was immediately set upon by earlier residents of Kalaupapa who stole what little he had as provisions. What terror that young boy must have felt.

The residents had arranged a luau for us and were very proud of the native dishes they had prepared. I have to admit I was somewhat nervous sitting down to the meal even though I knew the disease was no longer transmissible. As I looked around the table, I could see the terrible scars left by this dreaded disease, and I wondered about the emotional scars that didn't show. As we prepared to leave, Senator Akaka, who made the visit with me, started to sing a beautiful, traditional Hawaiian song. Everyone gathered around in a circle, and we all joined hands and voices as best we could. Hands missing fingers joined with our healthy hands as we swayed to the music. I thought of the difficult life these gentle people had led, yet this patriotic song of Hawaii still stirred them. I was unashamed of the tears of emotion that clouded my sight.

Senator Akaka and I had spent much of the day visiting the facilities at Kalaupapa and talking with the residents. We found that they were badly in need of a fire engine as the one they had was practically useless. I made a mental note to someway, somehow find them a fire engine as quickly as possible when we got back to Washington. Through the efforts of my assistant, Jim Parham, and his connections with Senator Akaka's staff and the military, we found them an engine and made the arrangements to transport it to Kalaupapa—no small task. I felt grateful that our NPS people were willing and able to do something for the residents of Kalaupapa.

Part Two

Management Philosophy
&
Goals of the NPS

6

Managing the NPS—The Internal Organization

With all the vast acreage, the natural wonders, and the historic and cultural treasures of the national park system, an NPS director's success or failure will depend on how he or she manages people. People cause things to happen or not to happen. If you can get a workforce in excess of fourteen thousand people moving in the same general direction, it is amazing what it can accomplish. But if that workforce is badly splintered and heading off in incompatible directions, it can make a total mess of the organization's goals.

With this in mind, I wanted to let the NPS workforce know where I was headed at the outset. Before my appointment was officially announced, I holed up in an office with a typewriter in an effort to lay out guiding principles to use in starting my new job. As I've mentioned, I had read a great deal of NPS history and talked with people who had been major players in NPS thinking over the years. I wanted to hit the ground running and felt that I should commit myself on paper to goals and objectives I envisioned for the parks during my term of office. I gave the task much thought.

I named the list my "Philosophical Thoughts." [see *Appendix I*] When I reviewed and numbered them for publication I discovered I had listed thirteen goals or guiding principles. I wondered if I shouldn't think of one more to get by the old superstition. No, I liked what I had written and wouldn't change it. Imagine my surprise when I realized that I was to be the thirteenth director of the Park Service!

I've included that early "think piece" for your reference in the appendix of this book. In reviewing those thoughts while writing this chapter, I'm pleased to see that I remained consistent to those principles throughout my four years.

No one person can possibly manage the Park Service. That must be why they give the top job the title of director. You can direct and lead, but a director would make a terrible mistake to try to get involved in the daily decisions at all levels of the organization.

I have always taken the view that a good leader should surround himself with good people, clearly set out a path to follow, then get out of the way and allow them to function. Give people a chance to prove they can do a good job until they prove they can't. Sure they will make mistakes, but so will you. In a world of rapid change, if you want decisions made you must expect mistakes. As long as the mistakes are honest and don't begin to show up as a pattern, I almost always give people a second, if not a third, chance.

The field staff of the Park Service is under the direct leadership of ten regional directors, who have great autonomy in running the parks within their regions. Each of my regional directors was different. Some were outstanding, as you would expect of people who had gone through a rigorous, competitive process to get their jobs. Others, who either resisted making decisions for fear of making mistakes or made decisions without regard for their repercussions on other regions and the entire organization, required more guidance and counseling. I had to adapt my management style to fit each regional director. Of course there were regional jealousies and competition for funds, but that was to be expected. Fortunately, with one or two exceptions, our field management team was strong and stayed on throughout my four years.

Some NPS regions are tougher to manage than others. I'm not going to set off a range war by naming one over the other, but I will say that the commonly held belief that the big western parks are the toughest challenge is no longer true, if it ever was. Many of the western parks have been around for a long time and their management patterns are pretty well set. All regions have tough issues, of course, but the parks in the East, Midwest, and South have taken on a higher profile in recent years. The creation of new park sites in these regions and the need to put management plans in place for them makes the country east of the Mississippi at least as challenging for Park Service personnel as the country to the west.

The day-to-day decisions in the parks are made by the park superintendents, who report to the regional directors for guidance. I think these people closest to the action generally have the best feel for the decisions that need to be made, and they are getting paid to make those decisions. On occasion they need to send the decision up the line to be made. Of course, this removal of decision making to a higher level makes it harder for those who might want to appeal.

A great deal of common sense comes in handy when trying to determine the proper level for decision making. I had some superintendents who went way beyond their authority in making decisions and some who were afraid to make any decision. Management training programs can help in these areas, but a lot depends on the common sense of the superintendent.

A question I often ask myself and urge others to ask is, "Can the decision pass the red-face test?" That is, will you be comfortable that you've done the right thing when you see your decision dissected on television or in the papers the next day, or will you be embarrassed? Notice I didn't say anything about the legality of the decision. I think you start off with the premise that you will make a legal decision to the best of your ability; then you search for the "right" decision. If you find that the right decision is not legally authorized, you have a problem. If you feel very strongly about it, it's time to go to Congress and get the law changed.

The tough decisions are rarely black or white. The decisions in shades of gray are what turn your hair shades of gray.

Reporting directly to me, in addition to the regional directors, were a deputy director and six associate directors in the Washington office. There are associate directors for operations, planning and development, natural resources, cultural resources, management systems, and budget and administration. Their staff responsibilities relate to Park Service areas and activities throughout the nation.

The deputy, associate and regional directors are all senior executives and are paid more than $100,000 annually for their services. Generally I would say they are underpaid compared with executives with comparable responsibilities in the private sector, but they are the highest-paid career employees in the Park Service. Since they're being paid to make decisions, it's important to let them do so rather than micro-manage them from the top.

As you might expect, their decisions are not always popular with the public or other Park Service personnel. I would often get anonymous mail complaining about one decision or another. Usually I would ignore anonymous letters unless I saw a pattern developing where employees were afraid to sign a letter for fear of retaliation. If I saw such a pattern I would investigate the situation, but I would much rather have had a signed letter of complaint. When you look into the single unsigned complaint letter, you will usually find a disgruntled ex-employee who wasn't doing the job and has moved on.

I have always believed in trusting people until they prove they can't be trusted. It doesn't take long to find out whether a person is trustworthy. I can even work with those I don't trust. I just have to adjust my management style. The leader who says he or she is always consistent in management style is either mistaken or misguided. Some employees need a pat on the back every day. Some need detailed instructions. Others can operate with a broad agenda from the boss. Different strokes for different folks—that's what makes people management so interesting and challenging.

At one time in my career I would get memos from a staffer who would start by noting that he was still at his desk at 10:30 P.M. and needed me to review one thing or another. Evidently he was trying to impress me with his long hours on the job, but his memos had the opposite effect. After putting up with this for a while, I finally called him in to tell him there was something wrong if he couldn't get his work done reasonably close to within normal business hours. Either he didn't have the ability to handle his job or he wasn't making good use of his time. As I suspected, he had been socializing around the halls of the office most of the day and not starting any meaningful work until everyone else had gone home. I changed his management style.

I believe that good leaders are able to adjust to the situations in which they find themselves. As director of the Indiana Department of Natural Resources I had resource management responsibilities extending beyond parks and environmental interests, much like the secretary of the Interior at the federal level. I had to weigh all options between competing interests and make decisions based on what I felt was in the overall public interest. As NPS director, even though I was operating on the national stage, I was more narrowly focused. I needed to represent the park or environmental viewpoint and let someone else, like the Bureau of Mines or the Bureau of Land Management, stick up for coal mining or cattle grazing.

Many battles involving the Park Service were over environmental protection issues, since the parks are such visible symbols of our commitment to the environment. Although the issues were often unclear, and good science upon which to base decisions was lacking, I felt we should take a strong pro-environment position to show the country and the world that we cared. I knew that compromises would need to be forged at the secretarial level—maybe as high as cabinet meetings. By the time we were into the second year of the Bush administration, I am happy to say that the NPS was present when the arguments to Secretary Lujan were made. We didn't always win but we had a place at the table—something that often hadn't happened in recent years.

While I was committed to the park and environmental protection agenda, I retained my strong belief in individual rights, including property rights. For example, I have tried to avoid taking private land by condemnation unless no other course of compromise is available. When I arrived in Washington I found stacks of unprocessed condemnation actions piled up behind the desk of the acting assistant secretary for Fish and Wildlife and Parks, Becky Dunlop. The documents had been stacking up long before she got to the job and continued to stack up on her watch. It was a massive job to sort through those condemnation actions to separate those that were critical to the mission of the agency from those that were of marginal importance.

It was a great relief to learn that many of the people against whom we were processing condemnation suits were not only willing but in some cases anxious to sell to us. The only sticking point was price. Often the landowner had decided that the only way to agree on a price was to have a court-ordered appraiser make the decision. These were essentially friendly suits. Often the sellers were trying to settle an estate or had other personal reasons for wanting to sell. It wasn't until we got a new assistant secretary that I began to move that huge backlog of condemnation suits on to the courtroom.

✳

Reporters will often scream that a decision has been politically influenced. My answer to that is yes, decisions are often politically influenced. That's the form of government we have in the United States. Those in the bureaucracy are not elected by the people and don't have the ultimate authority. It's their job to give the best information possible to our politically elected officials because that's where the responsibility ultimately rests. That's why we have elections.

I don't want this statement to sound overly naive. I've been around long enough to recognize when a decision not in the best interests of the country is being driven by one special interest group or another. When I found that to be the case, it was my job to convince other elected officials that a bad decision was being forced on us. If the elected officials didn't agree with me and the decision, in my judgment, was extremely critical, then I should be prepared to resign and become a private citizen. A good leader knows when and how to pick his fights. He can't put his back to the wall on every issue or he'll become known as the person who cries wolf and will lose his effectiveness.

A good example is the case of the "vision document" dealing with the management of the greater Yellowstone ecosystem. There are some aspects of that situation that are still tied up in the courts, but I can speak to the issue generally as it relates to decision making in the parks and across park lines.

I was aware that our Rocky Mountain regional director and a number of the U.S. Forest Service supervisors who had responsibility for Forest Service land surrounding Yellowstone National Park had been working on a plan to do a better job of coordinating their activities within the Yellowstone ecosystem. They had been working on it for years, long before I became director. The idea of better cooperation made good sense and I was supportive of the effort in principle, not having seen the details.

I had talked with Dale Robertson, chief of the Forest Service, and he and I agreed that it was a good idea to spell out some of the ways we might do a better job of cooperating within the region, but we didn't see the need for this to take the form of a command from Washington. A memorandum of understanding among the federal land managers in the area might be preferable.

I found the first draft of the "vision document" to be entirely too wordy and not something that could be instructive to the public. My advice was to rewrite it with the intent of having a more readable, understandable document—one that could be used in our educational programs both inside and outside the park. Our regional director and the Forest Service people took this suggestion and began a rewrite. Dale and I both told our people to do their best to reach consensus. We would have a conference-telephone call in which Dale and I would make the final decisions on any remaining areas of disagreement.

Some months went by with various drafts floating around between the Forest Service and the Park Service before the conference call was set up. Our regional director, a Forest Service supervisor and a staff person from each agency who had been assigned to work on the project were included along with Dale and me. I had read the latest draft and was satisfied that it was much more readable; many of the typical buzzwords used by the professional planners had been dropped, much to my relief. It looked like a document that a visitor could pick up in our visitor center to get a better idea of our management philosophy.

Surprisingly, there were not many issues for Dale and me to settle—maybe four or five—and the more our people explained them the more it became apparent that these were not unsolvable problems. In fact, common sense seemed to lead them to compromise language without Dale or me having to say much of anything. Our regional director made some of the best suggestions and took notes on the final wording. I thought everything was coming up roses.

In a matter of days this whole subject became headlines in newspapers across the country. Cries of political interference were coming from everywhere. Special interest groups on one end of the spectrum or the other began the war chant on how their rights were being trampled. I couldn't believe it! All we had was an agreement to coordinate our decisions in a better fashion than we had in the past. Who or what was stirring up this highly emotional storm of protest was beyond me. All sorts of ills were being ascribed to the document and the process by which it was put together. Consumptive users—miners, loggers and livestock grazers—were sure it was intended as a slap in their faces. The environmental groups were sure that political types had ordered us to gut the document, because it was shorter than the original draft. I reminded them that the Gettysburg Address, which was pretty effective, was less than one page long and took less than two minutes to deliver.

To check my sanity I decided to have an associate director known for his good sense read both documents. I asked him to tell me how much the shorter version had lost in terms of intent from the longer, more wordy draft. His answer was what I expected. He thought the intent was still evident and the substance was still there. I felt this justified my feeling that I was dealing with years of paranoia on both sides of the issue with all the fussing going on. I really didn't find much substance in the arguments of either side.

Was the vision document a back-to-the-wall, do-or-die issue? I didn't think so at the time, and on reflection I still don't think so. Was it politically hot? You bet. I can't begin to quantify what all the fuss cost the American taxpayers. One committee in Congress must have spent well into the millions of dollars on an investigation that proved nothing. The issue became political in the worst way, and copiers are still running in Washington to substantiate positions taken on it one way or another.

As a side note, the congressman who led the charge in the investigation was defeated in the next election before he could culminate his efforts, so his staff leaked a report—full of inaccuracies—without the approval of the responsible congressional committee. They had too much money and pride tied up in their investigation to simply let it die. Speaking of politics in the system, I was asked to testify before the committee but was told I couldn't be represented by our Interior lawyers and my testimony would be behind closed doors. I agreed to testify but insisted that it be out in the open with opportunity for the press to attend. I offered to testify under those conditions on at least three occasions. It was clear to me that the committee staff didn't want anyone to testify in public if there was a chance that the testimony wouldn't agree with their conclusions.

✳

As in any widespread organization, communications were often difficult. Our time zones started in the East with the Virgin Islands and stretched to war memorials in Guam and Saipan. I got together with the regional and associate directors on a planned basis, but it was time-consuming and expensive to bring people together frequently.

We installed electronic mail during my four years, and that was a big help. With the electronic mail, all parks could easily correspond with Washington, the regional offices and each other. In my last year we linked Washington to the regional offices through a sophisticated television system. I could get face-to-face with the regional directors via this system when discussing such things as their annual evaluations. Before, regional office people had always come to Washington to presents drafts of their planning studies. A presentation typically involved five or six people with lots of charts and graphs. This expensive travel could now be avoided through the use of the television system. If used well, it will be a big money saver for the Park Service.

One of the organizational trends that bothered me the most was the declining number of our interpretative rangers (rangers dedicated to public education) as emphasis had to be shifted more and more to law enforcement. I don't have a ready solution to the problem. I believe strongly that people should have the right to feel safe in the parks, but I hated to see our educational efforts suffer with the bigger dollars going to enforcement. I guess we all might agree on this issue.

The Park Service has had the reputation of being one big happy family, and to some extent that is true. There is a great spirit of togetherness among park employees and a can-do attitude that is rare among government agencies. But it's getting harder and harder to hold the family together as the park system and its workforce grow and diversify. Some people view themselves as only interested in natural parks, while others in cultural parks think they don't get any respect. The sheer size of the system makes annual reunions impossible. There was a day when a director knew most of the people in the organization. I spent as much time as I could in the field and tried to meet as many people as possible.

It was always my philosophy that the field is where "the rubber meets the road." As far as the public's impression is concerned, the park maintenance person cutting the grass or cleaning the visitor center may be just as important as the park ranger. After all, the maintenance person may be the only NPS employee a park visitor will see. I encouraged the creation of a system-wide employee orientation program so that all our people would feel comfortable meeting and dealing with the public.

The family concept is still there, but some of the cousins are getting hard to find. It is an era I hate to see die.

I want to conclude this chapter with a statement of appreciation for a longtime NPS family member, George Hartzog. George is nationally and internationally known and admired in park circles. He is one of the brightest men and most gifted speakers I have ever met. As a respected former director (1964-1972) his opinion carries special weight, and I know he was often called by the press, park employees or other interested parties to see if he would second-guess me. To his credit George never entered into these traps, and I always appreciated his support. If he had a problem, he called me and we talked quite frankly. He was and is a great supporter of the Park Service and a true gentleman as well.

7

The Seventy-Fifth Anniversary & the Vail Agenda

On August 25, 1991, the National Park Service celebrated its seventy-fifth anniversary. The 1916 act of Congress that created the bureau contained a two-pronged mission statement, still in effect, mandating both conservation and public enjoyment of park resources:

> *The service thus established shall promote and regulate the use of the Federal areas known as national parks, monuments, and reservations... by such means and measures as conform to the fundamental purpose of the said parks, monuments, and reservations, which purpose is to conserve the scenery and the natural and historic objects and the wild life therein and to provide for the enjoyment of the same in such manner and by such means as will leave them unimpaired for the enjoyment of future generations.*

This dual purpose set up a natural tension within the Park Service that endures to this day. Scholars and practitioners alike have debated for years the agency's mission and how best to advance it. Are the parks primarily for preservation or for recreation? Are these objectives compatible? Is it possible to conserve park resources "unimpaired" while providing for their enjoyment?

You can chase your tail all day on this topic. For me, it wasn't that complicated. Common sense told me you had to protect the resources or there wouldn't be any resources to protect. Protection had to come first, but protection didn't necessarily mean absolute preservation. The law directs the agency not to "preserve" but to "conserve," and conservation has traditionally involved wise use. Of course, there are fragile and irreplaceable resources for which a strict preservation approach is essential.

More times than not, common sense will lead you to compromises allowing resources to be enjoyed while being conserved. However, the key to understanding the art of compromise is knowing when not to compromise. That can only come with knowledge and experience.

Before becoming its director I had studied the history of the Park Service, met with some of its key people over the years, and reached the conclusion that it lacked a strong commitment to science. What science capacity existed labored under suspicion and mistrust from other agencies, including sister bureaus within the Interior Department. There was even mistrust of its scientists within the agency itself.

I didn't see how you could make good management decisions if you didn't have good science. If you didn't know where the grizzly bear habitat was, how could you avoid it while building new campgrounds, roads, and other park facilities?

I made a strong commitment to science. I was especially interested in inventorying and monitoring the natural and cultural assets of the parks. I tripled the budget of a program called the geographic information system and called on the parks and regional offices to get their shoulders to the wheel in this effort.

In simple terms, the Geographic Information System, or GIS, is a computerized method of storing and retrieving information in a way that allows you to graphically analyze a decision, based on the gathered data, before making it. It would have been nice to have this system before the huge *Exxon Valdez* oil spill in Alaska. Without an adequate understanding of what we had, it was difficult to prove what we had lost.

While the whole area of science and resource protection got a big boost during my tenure, to look at the big picture we had to look further than the science program as we had known it. We had to do some serious thinking about the direction of the Park Service going into the next century. The seventy-fifth anniversary year gave us a good excuse to do this.

Mrs. Bush agreed to serve as our honorary chairperson for the seventy-fifth anniversary. She hosted a particularly important afternoon tea at the White House for a number of top industry leaders that gave us a chance to do a little "soft sell" on our objectives. To our surprise she asked if her husband could attend. We were thrilled to have the president make a good pitch as to why the parks were so important to the country.

When the president left, Mrs. Bush returned to their private quarters and came back wearing the ranger hat we had given her when making her an honorary ranger. She said the president didn't think she should wear it inside the house, but now that he had gone she wanted to show her pride at becoming an honorary ranger—an honor the Park Service does not bestow lightly. The White House event paid off in financial support and the loan of key people from America's private sector for our effort.

To show my strong commitment to the seventy-fifth anniversary year, I asked Herb Cables, our very capable deputy director, to devote his time to leading us in our anniversary events. Observances took place throughout the parks during the year, but the most important event was not a celebration as much as a commitment to internal review and strategic thinking. It culminated in a hard-hitting symposium in October where we hammered out a plan for the future. The official name for the plan was "National Parks For the 21st Century," but almost everyone referred to it as the Vail Agenda.

I was a little concerned that we were holding our symposium at Vail, Colorado, because the image of the ski resort is not exactly the image of the Park Service. But we were there in the off-season, the central location and access via Denver were good, and the prices were right. We couldn't have booked into one of our NPS concession hotels at that time of year without displacing all our guests.

From the start I wanted it made clear that this was not to be a whitewash of past practices by the Park Service. I wanted the agenda to be wide open and I wanted help from the private and academic world for this introspection.

Henry Diamond, a highly respected conservationist who has held numerous positions of importance to the park users of America, agreed to chair the Vail meeting and lead us through all the preliminary meetings that would place an agenda on the table for us to consider at the final symposium. These preliminary meetings were tough work sessions designed to give everyone a say. Our steering committee, listed in the appendix of this book, was made up of outstanding leaders such as former ambassador to Australia Bill Lane from the private sector, and our own Bill Briggle, who was a real stalwart throughout this process. Alan Rubin, president of the National Park Foundation, provided us with three valuable contributions: brains, money and friendship.

The World Wildlife Fund and the Conservation Fund contributed financial support and talented leaders such as Pat Noonan to help us think through our future. Much of the activity was orchestrated by Harvard's Kennedy School of Government.

Herb Cables and Bill Briggle led us through this tiring but rewarding exercise. They had plenty of help from within as we called on all levels of the NPS organization to get as broad a range of thinking as possible. I honestly don't know how we could have thrown our loop any wider to include differing views. We offered opportunities to be involved to all who would be willing—friend or foe—to take part in the activity.

The end result is a 137-page document that is the blueprint for the direction of the National Park Service into the next century. It is not a Republican blueprint. It is not a Democratic blueprint. It is a Park Service blueprint with strong support from all ranks of interested park employees and many public and private individuals and organizations. I believe it is the strongest statement of consensus ever put together on the Park Service, and I hope future directors will use it to guide their decisions in leading this great public agency.

The report contains six strategic objectives and more than 140 specific recommendations as to how to achieve them. I won't attempt to duplicate the report in this chapter, but I do want to point to a few highlights.

Strategic Objective 1:

Resource Stewardship and Protection basically reaffirms that you first have to protect the resources for which the parks have been established. This was an objective nearly everyone could support.

I could recall a very zealous budget analyst from my state park days who pointed out that we could cut down and sell all the beautiful walnut trees we had in one of our parks and pay for the operation of the entire state park system. I said that if we were to do that we would no longer have a state park but a state parking lot.

Among the many suggestions as to how we might better accomplish this objective was one I had been working on with Associate Director Deny Galvin. We were in search of a program that would allow recognition and help for areas suggested for national park status that do not quite reach the standard for inclusion in the national system. Often these areas are of considerable value and deserve protection and public support. Deny and I were looking for a mechanism that would allow the Park Service to provide technical and planning services to other levels of government and, in some cases, funds that would flow through the Park Service to assist. We didn't want a long-term federal commitment of funds and discussed a plan that would not extend federal financial support for more than five years.

We called this proposal the American Heritage Area program as a working title. I think the concept has great merit. While it might place a burden of providing technical assistance and advice on the Park Service, the cost to the federal government will be less in the long run by allowing state and local governments and possibly private partners to maintain their proper role in the provision of parks and services to the public. When I left we were actively shopping the proposal around state and local government leaders to see what they thought.

Strategic Objective 2:

Access and Enjoyment focuses on the importance of providing access to our great park sites while respecting the first objective of resource protection.

One of the specific recommendations here is that the Park Service should minimize the development of facilities within park boundaries to the extent reasonable. This fits closely with my thoughts on the possible uses of Forest Service and Bureau of Land Management land outside park boundaries.

Both of these agencies are struggling to redefine their missions. Their original missions have taken a beating for a number of years and the beating is growing stronger. Let's face it: The campaign to preserve the forest habitat of the spotted owl in the Pacific Northwest is just an example of a much stronger movement to limit timber production on federal lands across this country. The Forest Service might not stop all timbering, but it will have to radically reduce its current practices. The old timber interests have come up against formidable foes, and mining and grazing interests on Forest Service land are likely to meet the same end. As a result, the Forest Service is going to become a more recreationally oriented agency in the future.

The same holds true for the BLM, which manages more that 250 million acres in this country. Although some dismiss its holdings as what was left over after the Park Service and the Forest Service got first choice, BLM has some great land in key places, including the great desert areas of Southern California. The BLM is also seeing the handwriting on the wall and is increasing its promotion of outdoor recreation.

I view these changes as good news for the Park Service. To the extent that the other land managing agencies can accommodate the more active outdoor recreation activities, pressures for these activities on park lands will be eased. The fast-growing sport of off-road bicycling can be served in less-sensitive BLM and Forest Service areas. If new campgrounds or other overnight accommodations need to be built for visitors to Yellowstone or Yosemite, build them on neighboring Forest Service land and provide shuttle service to key park destinations.

I foresee a continued shrinking in the distinctive differences among the land managing agencies, a trend I named "the blurring of the lines." I think our resources and people will be better served as a result.

Another recommendation under this objective is to encourage visitor services development in gateway cities outside the parks. In this regard I would encourage park superintendents and staff members to become active participants in local organizations so that they become well-respected community members. They should avoid becoming perceived as "parkies" who come running out to protest community decisions at the last minute. NPS people need to be working with local communities to see not only that park interests are well served but that park neighbors understand and appreciate those interests.

Strategic Objective 3:

Education and Interpretation reinforces the importance of educational and interpretive programs. As more and more of our citizens live in the big cities and are not exposed to the national parks, it will become more difficult to maintain the support of our elected leadership in furthering park objectives without a strong outreach effort. I'm reminded of the story of the shopper who says, "Why should I care about the dairy farmer? I get my milk at the grocery store."

There are a lot of recommendations that spin out of this objective. You can't do a good job of educating unless you have the facts. This means the science system and the inventorying and monitoring of resources must improve. Thankfully this effort is under way, but it must get stronger and pervade the entire park system.

Strategic Objective 4:

Proactive Leadership basically says that the Park Service needs to take the initiative in shaping its destiny. I couldn't agree more.

One of the specific recommendations here was creation of an office of strategic planning. I'm happy to say that we established that office and had it in place before the ink was dry on the report.

The Park Service had become a captive of micro-management by Congress and, to some extent, others in the executive branch. I think we greatly improved that situation in the four years of the Bush administration. I can honestly say that I was given the opportunity to run the agency. That doesn't mean I always got my way, but I got my chance to be heard.

There were days when I didn't feel in control because the tune was being called by too many outside interests. We weren't anticipating; we were reacting. Putting out one brushfire after another seemed to consume us. Of course, you can't avoid reacting to emergencies, but our creation of the new strategic planning office was a step in the right direction.

Some people criticized me for putting the office in Denver rather than close to me in Washington, but I did so for a specific purpose. If the office were down the hall from me I would likely have grabbed it to work on the emergency of the day. I wanted to keep it away from that brushfire mentality—thus the decision to put it anywhere but Washington.

71

Strategic Objective 5:

Science and Research addresses a particular interest of mine, as I've said earlier. I won't spend a great deal of time rehashing this topic, even though I'm especially proud of my accomplishments here. We more than doubled the science and resource protection budget in my four years. Doubling the funds does not always double the commitment, although I hope this is the result. The jury is still out on much of this, as it takes time to evaluate a growing research commitment.

A proper research program that is heavily into inventorying and monitoring the conditions in the parks can be invaluable not only to the parks but to the entire country. Using the old "canary in the coal mine" analogy, parks can be used to detect subtle and not-so-subtle changes in our environment. They can serve as barometers of the nation's health. I encouraged other agencies to use the parks to "sniff the air and taste the water" of this country.

As an example, I believe the quality of water that flows to Everglades National Park in southern Florida is important not only to the park but to every resident in the area. When a Florida panther there dies with a high concentration of lead in its liver, that concerns me. Where did all this lead come from? What was the panther eating and drinking? What are southern Floridians eating and drinking? The connection is there and is important to our environmental and personal health.

Strategic Objective 6:

Professionalism relates to the capability of NPS personnel. There is no degree requirement to become a ranger in the Park Service. There is a degree requirement to do similar work for the Forest Service. The Forest Service is better able to recruit and maintain a professional workforce. In fact, most park rangers have degrees, but the wide range of activities a ranger must perform has made it difficult to set a specific degree requirement.

Personally, I think the best academic program for most park people is one leading to a good liberal arts degree. Rangers are called upon to be and do many things. By and large, they are "people people." They spend much of their time dealing with people, in both positive and negative contexts. The parks have long been mirrors of society, and unfortunately this is true in the areas of crime prevention and control. Obviously you need special training for law enforcement work, but a good liberal arts background is likely to be a big plus.

Another plus is a second language. More than 40 percent of those coming to some of our parks are from other nations. With this massive influx of international visitors, it is becoming more and more important that park people be bilingual.

The bottom line is that the people who work for the Park Service are its greatest asset. We are not adequately paying them, housing them or giving them fair and equitable treatment. It is one thing to hire young, idealistic college graduates with a great love of the parks and ask them to take part of their pay in sunsets. But as they have growing families with needs and the dream of educating their kids, we have to think of maintaining reasonable standards of living for these dedicated public servants. We aren't doing that now!

The Vail Agenda is a great call to arms. The ball is rolling and the momentum is growing. I would urge the leadership from the president to the Congress to the secretary of the Interior to commit themselves to it. It is the future of the National Park Service.

Part Three

✤

Money, Power & Politics

8

Dealing with Congress

Imagine my surprise when I got to Washington and found that the National Park Service wasn't in the executive branch of government. Coming from a strong executive branch state like Indiana, I expected to be in charge of running the bureau. Instead I found Congress and, worse yet, congressional staffs running it.

I was absolutely amazed to find staffers on Capitol Hill trying to decide whom I would hire and when I would hire them—even threatening to cut specific people out of our budget unless I cooperated in keeping their pets on the payroll. They are into micro-management big time. I don't think this was just because I was part of a Republican administration confronting a Democratic Congress. From what I have read, Secretary of the Interior Bruce Babbitt of the Clinton administration can't believe the interference he gets from Congress on a daily basis in running his department.

A staffer from a western senator's office called my executive assistant, Jim Parham, and chewed him out for at least twenty minutes. He went on and on about how angry his boss, the senator, was with me. There were threats about cutting our budget, stopping bills we had an interest in, and so on.

It was puzzling to me why this senator would be so upset. I hadn't even met him. That night I got my chance. Senator Richard Lugar of Indiana had invited us over for some sort of reception, and guess who I saw standing near the hors d'oeuvres? The irate young staffer's boss. I decided to meet the problem head on.

I introduced myself to the senator and told him I'd heard he was very angry with the Park Service and me. I said I hoped I could get an appointment on his schedule to work out his concerns. He looked confused.

Finally he said, "Hell, I don't have any idea what this might be about. Forget it—and let me buy you a drink."

Wouldn't you know, the next day the same staffer called back and resumed his harangue. He took off just where he had stopped the day before. Jim played along and listened for about ten minutes, then told the staffer, "We were with your boss last night for more than two hours and offered to meet with him to iron out our differences. He said he had no idea what you were talking about and not to worry!" It was great fun to catch the staffer playing the role of junior senator, but the sad thing is that it happens all too often.

Over the years there have been shifts of power between the executive and legislative branches. Usually these shifts balance out one another over time, but I'm not so sure that the Congress will yield any of the middle ground it has seized for itself in recent years. There are a number of reasons why the Congress has reached beyond its constitutional role and is usurping the power of the presidency.

C-SPAN has come along, and members of Congress are enamored with the hours of free exposure they are getting across the nation on a daily basis. When television first started covering the Washington scene, technology and time limited most coverage to the nation's prime spokesman—the president. Now, with twenty-four-hour cable coverage, there isn't enough "quality" news to fill the airwaves, so we viewers are treated to full speeches by freshmen congressmen and -women we once would have never heard of but who are now coming into our living rooms hoping to catch our eye in case they decide to run for higher office sometime.

Another major factor that leads Congress toward domination is the size of its staff as compared with twenty and thirty years ago. Staff sizes have doubled, even tripled. With such large staffs, members have the ability to become semi-experts on everything. I guarantee that a number of them were pretty sure they could run the National Park Service better than I or any other director in recent memory.

And you can't ignore the most obvious reason that people point to when trying to explain why Congress stays in Washington so much longer than in the past: air conditioning. Without air conditioning we would probably have a seven- or eight-month Congress. With the comfort of air conditioning, members can stay all year, visit their states and districts only briefly, and try to run the executive branch and the courts as well.

In Indiana the state legislature is allowed to meet for sixty days every two years. The oft-repeated remark is that the citizens would be better off if the legislature were allowed to meet two days every sixty years. There is something to be said for a citizen legislature.

There's a big push for term limits for members of Congress, as we have for the president. In theory I favor this, but nothing will be accomplished if the same congressional staff stays year after year. It is the staff that writes the bills; it is the staff that works until the wee hours of the morning fine-tuning the budget for the members; it is the staff that holds the institutional memory and knows where and how to hide bill language that suits its agenda; and it is the staff that leads the charge on micro-managing the executive branch. Unless something is done to curtail the growing power of the unelected members of Congress, term limits will not help much.

I'm not sure when Congress first started to run the Park Service, but I know the trend accelerated during the Reagan years. President Reagan and his staff had this funny idea that if you didn't ask the Congress for money, you wouldn't get any. He was trying to hold down the deficit—a worthy objective. But the strategy didn't work as far as the Park Service was concerned. The president's budget request would be low and the members of Congress would start loading up the Park Service's appropriation like a Christmas tree. The pork barrel or, rather, the park barrel, was so full it was slopping over. We couldn't build things as fast as they gave us money to build them.

You'd think that as a bureau director I'd be pleased with getting a bigger budget than requested. I would have been, but they gave us a whole lot of stuff we didn't want. We didn't have enough resources to take care of the parks and buildings we had—and they were loading us up with what, in many cases, were local economic development projects, thus thinning the blood of the National Park Service.

Many of the new parks and projects approved by Congress were unworthy of NPS status or support but got voted in anyway. As a result, the quality of the national park system suffered because this put additional financial demands on a program that was already badly underfunded. As I will discuss later, we were and are not taking care of our greatest natural and cultural assets—the Grand Canyons, the Yellowstones, the Everglades, and historic sites such as Independence Hall—yet we are spending hundreds of millions of dollars on what can best be described as local or regional economic development projects.

As I mentioned in the introduction, this did not just happen recently. From the early Park Service days, those concerned about maintaining the national significance of the park system were not always able to defeat substandard park proposals. But in the 1970s, under the leadership of California Congressman Phil Burton, the House subcommittee responsible for authorizing parks became known as the park-of-the-month club. What were Burton's motives? Was he trying to get everything under the umbrella of NPS in the short term, figuring the long-term issue—namely, who was going to pay for it—would iron itself out later? Or was Burton a skillful park-barrel manipulator?

Granted, there were worthy as well as unworthy parks that came into the system under Burton. But the Presidio of San Francisco is one that will impact NPS operations forever. Burton may have had a premonition when he tagged a few lines on to the 1972 law authorizing Golden Gate National Recreation Area. He arranged it so the Presidio would become part of the recreation area when no longer needed for military purposes, as is now the case.

The Presidio is one of the great pieces of property in the world, sitting right at the end of the Golden Gate Bridge. It has spectacular vistas and is extremely interesting from a historic and architectural point of view. But how do we find the right use of the property, and how do we keep it in a parklike condition without spending huge sums of taxpayers' money to operate? All kinds of figures have been kicked around—I was told that the NPS might expect to spend $40 million a year just for operating expenses. That is more than double the annual operations budget of Yellowstone, which is badly underfunded at about $18 million.

Initial plans call for renting many of the Presidio's buildings to private industry in order to recover much of the cost of operation. Time will tell whether there is enough interest in the commercial real estate business of San Francisco to make this plan work. I hope the planners and politicians can make it work. I especially hope they can make it work without starving the rest of the national park system.

Another project that people were either fiercely for or fiercely against during my time in office was Congressman Joe McDade's Steamtown National Historic Site at Scranton, Pennsylvania. A park unit with a collection of old steam rail engines, a roundhouse that is being converted into a museum, and other features including steam train rides, Steamtown is a charming but very costly project—we're talking something in the $60 million range.

To complicate matters, Joe, a high-ranking member of the House Appropriations Committee, initially shoved the project through the appropriations process without first going through the authorizing committees in Congress. Even powerful congressmen are supposed to get projects authorized before putting funds in the budget to start construction.

I want to make it clear that Joe McDade is not the only congressman who has bypassed the authorizing committees. Other unauthorized projects in other states and congressional districts have become the beneficiaries of federal appropriations amid the horse-trading that goes on in the final hours of passing budget bills. But those other projects were not simultaneously brought into the national park system to become perpetual burdens on the federal taxpayer.

That Steamtown should be a national historic site is doubtful. As an economic development project Steamtown does have great potential to attract tourists and to benefit the local and regional economy. But I don't think it's of national park stature.

Congressman John Murtha's American Industrial Heritage Project in western Pennsylvania has much the same flavor. Big dollars have been and will be spent before this project, linking a number of historic industrial sites together in a nine-county area, is complete. Is it an interesting collection of sites interpreting America's industrial growth? Without a doubt. Should it be funded by the Park Service or become part of the national park system? That answer is debatable.

As chairman of the Senate Appropriations Committee, Senator Robert Byrd of West Virginia has been a strong and well-placed advocate for NPS involvement in his state. Certainly there are many things to do in "almost heaven." The problem is that Senator Byrd wants the federal government to pay for buying and fixing up many of its sites. In my mind, the New River Gorge has national park qualities—especially if the NPS concentrates on telling the story of coal mining, labor unions, company towns and other aspects of its important history. The national significance of another project he has underway at Wheeling, West Virginia, is less evident. Certainly Wheeling was a gateway to the West: When the settlers saw the mighty Ohio River heading westward from Wheeling, they had to decide whether to stay or go. It may be that parts of Wheeling deserve national park recognition, but I don't believe the Park Service should be expected to fund the economic development that the project's proponents are seeking.

Congressman Bob Davis, with late support from Senator Carl Levin of Michigan, added another slab of pork to the parks when he backed the addition of Keweenaw National Historic Park on the northern peninsula of Michigan. This park was established with the purpose of honoring the heritage of its copper mining industry. It has a lot of charm but I didn't think we should be adding it to the NPS list while we were hanging on by a fiscal shoestring.

Congressman Davis had been trying to get this area added into the NPS stable for a number of years. I finally agreed to visit the area to unveil the plaques placing the town of Quincy and the world's largest steam hoist, as well as Calumet, the site of one of the most productive copper mines in the world, on the National Register of Historic Places. It was hard for me to be less than supportive of this project as the people of the area were so enthusiastic about the possibility of having the area under park status.

There were a number of problems. The biggest was whether or not the area was sufficiently nationally significant to warrant park status. Some would say that if an area is granted National Historic Landmark status, then it automatically passes the significance test for becoming a national park. I don't agree. I believe the area or building must be eligible for national register status to qualify it for park consideration, but I don't think being on the national register automatically qualifies a candidate for park status.

Senator Robert Byrd of West Virginia tells the history of the New River Gorge as he and I join together in dedicating a beautiful new visitor center in the park.

Another problem was that there are acres of old mine tailings in the area that are draining into a small lake near Quincy. I had visions of our accepting this park and then being commanded by the Environmental Protection Agency to spend millions and millions of dollars to clean up the environmental problems of the past.

The old mine shaft was dug on a slant that ran more than six hundred feet under the surface. It was really an interesting place to see and to imagine what it was like in its heyday. I don't think I would have wanted to climb into those wooden cars that lowered those miners into the shaft day after day.

Quincy itself was a company town and a good example of what company towns were like in this country. It is still a very pleasant and interesting town that would make a nice tourist trip for those on an adventure to northern Michigan.

I don't know how Congressman Davis got support for this project. This is one that went right over my head and, like Congressman McDade's Steamtown, was moved along to national park status before going through the proper authorization channels in Congress. These things happen. I once had a congressman ask me how one of his colleagues got support of the Office of Management and Budget for a particular park project. I told him that I had heard a rumor that the congressman had given the administration support on an issue of great importance to the White House. "Darn," the congressman replied, "I only got two tickets to the Kennedy Center in exchange for *my* vote."

I will guarantee that you will enjoy a trip to Michigan's upper peninsula if you work it into your vacation plans. When you visit Quincy and learn of the history of the mining in the area, you can also work in a trip to Isle Royale, an existing, first-class national park just off the coast of the peninsula. The people will be glad to see you, and you will have an interesting look into the mining history of our country, but I still have doubts as to the national park stature of the copper country of the Keweenaw Peninsula.

Another area that was being pushed for consideration by the Connecticut congressional delegation was the studio of J. Alden Weir, a well-known impressionist painter. When the idea of making Weir's studio and the small acreage farm surrounding it a national historic site surfaced my antennae went up. Every state has a favorite painter and many of them would like to see the studios and homes of their painters or artists preserved. My own state of Indiana preserves the home of T. C. Steele. We think he was pretty special. Indiana, like many other states, struggles with finding the money to take care of Steele's home.

I could just see the flood of requests to preserve a painter's home in every state if we let the Weir site in. At a minimum I wanted what is called a theme study to identify the truly important American painters. I wasn't necessarily against the Weir Farm site but I wanted to know if we were picking the right painter's studio for inclusion. Frankly, I thought we were in danger of having to pick up the tab for the care and preservation of many artists' studios, and experience told me that properly taking care of art is expensive. I envisioned selecting a nationally known and respected panel of art experts to debate this topic and give us the advantage of their wisdom before we jumped off into this new direction.

I went so far as to ask leading art critics in the Washington, D.C., area what they thought of Weir's work. The general consensus was that he was good—very good—but not of the national stature of many of our finest painters. I called John Frohnmayer, director of the National Endowment for the Arts, to get an informal opinion. John gave me a rather lukewarm endorsement and the impression that there were other painters more worthy of consideration. I decided to ask the question more formally than my telephone survey so I could properly prepare my congressional testimony. Too late—the Connecticut delegation had already gotten to my art critics. All the written replies came back that Weir was the greatest thing since sliced bread and the result was that the J. Alden Weir Farm is now a part of the NPS.

Another project that gets huge appropriations is the Santa Monica Mountain Recreation Area. More than $148 million have been spent to purchase approximately twenty-thousand acres. Anticipated is another twelve-thousand-acre purchase for an additional cost of $50 million. In total, taxpayers will have about $200 million in the purchase of approximately thirty thousand acres. Those critical of NPS buying this very expensive Southern California land say that it is a project to protect the viewshed of the rich and famous. I wouldn't be that unkind in my assessment, but there is no doubt that the NPS could buy sizable portions of whole states for what they are paying for the land in the Santa Monica Mountains.

Of course, the people in that Los Angeles megalopolis need room to spill out into the countryside. Many of those kids in the urban area have never seen a park. More than a few have never set foot on anything that isn't concrete or asphalt and will never get the chance to see a Yellowstone or Yosemite. Where did the people go when the most recent earthquake scared them out of their houses? Back to the open land. Preserving this open land is important, so I support the Santa Monica Mountains Recreation Area as long as the NPS management does not let it turn into the playground of the rich, and works to help Los Angeles with the problems of the inner city.

While there are many areas worth additional mention, I can't help but think of the money that will be pouring into New Jersey over the next few years. It started rather innocently with the support of Senator Bill Bradley. It appeared that all Senator Bradley wanted was a survey of the places of interest in his state and some NPS advice on how to collectively present these attractions to the public—maybe some ideas on road signage, trails, etc. Thus was born the idea of the New Jersey Coastal Heritage Trail. My thought was that we would send up some tourism planners to give government officials in New Jersey a little advice in packaging their state attractively. No big deal and not a bad idea.

When I saw the rough draft of what our NPS staff planners wanted me to send to Congress I was amazed. What started out as a planning project would end up drawing the NPS deep into financial obligations to New Jersey. There was talk of buying up hundreds of acres of land, creating amenities for tourists, and generally handing over a plan to Congress that would legitimize an open checkbook to New Jersey for years. Our planners had gone way overboard based on a rather simple request. I don't know if Senator Bradley was aware how far his staff and the NPS staff had gone with this elaborate plan but if he did know, he wasn't complaining. This was an example of congressional staff and the NPS staff running amuck with pork park being the goal.

Our NPS planning staff was, at times, our own worst enemy.

National parks come in all sizes and shapes in California. Of course, California is loaded with natural beauty, and cultural and historical sites. Congressman Phil Burton had been kind to California and, of this writing, there are twenty NPS sites in the Golden State with a twenty-first looming gigantically on the horizon—the Presidio at San Francisco. All are not officially designated as parks. Some are memorials and monuments. For example, Death Valley is listed as a monument whereas Yosemite is listed as a park. You may ask, When is a property a park and when is it a monument? The answer is that it is whatever Congress says it is. When the Congress passes legislation, it designates what the area is to be called.

There is a little more logic to the process than it first appears. Generally speaking, a monument would be created based on a single significant feature; a park is expected to have a wider range of features. A park might be known for its mountains, its lakes and streams, its unique topography, or a combination of all of those things.

In California, the congressional delegation has been struggling for years as to what to do with the Mojave Desert—namely, whether or not to bring it to the natural park system. Much of the land belongs to the Bureau of Land Management (BLM) and has been managed as multiple-purpose-use land for years. The rules under which BLM manages land differ greatly from those of the NPS. I am not making a judgment on the way BLM operates except to say that the BLM footprint on the land is usually much heavier than you would find in the parks. Off-road vehicles are often allowed. Camping is often where you find it, not in designated campgrounds. Hunting is usually allowed and there may be grazing and mining in some areas. There has been a great deal of mining in the Mojave.

I tried to stay out of this long-standing feud in Southern California. We had Death Valley and Joshua Tree National Monuments in the area and I really wasn't interested in taking on a lot more land, especially land that has been heavily impacted by heavy multiple-use recreation. My compromise position was to expand Death Valley and Joshua Tree and to change their names from monuments to parks. It is one thing to create a park area and have the rules established from the very beginning. It is far more difficult to assume management of land that recreational users have used pretty much as they see fit. If the Congress decides that NPS must take over large chunks of the Mojave I guarantee you that much of the off-road-vehicle traffic will have to stop—and I don't think those people want to stop.

To inherit land with the long multiple-use philosophy practiced under BLM management would cause enforcement problems that would be mind-boggling, and I opted not to have the responsibility unless I had the capability to follow it up. Besides, if Congress wanted the Mojave treated differently, it could direct BLM to manage that vast acreage in a different way. I also happened to think that BLM, as an agency, was making strides toward a stronger environmental ethic and should be allowed to keep its "crown jewels" as a sign to encourage the evolving change in BLM management philosophy.

That fight is not over and won't be over, even if the Congress passes legislation. There is a lot of land in the Mojave and there are not enough rangers in the NPS to change the minds and lifestyles of the millions who use that land for recreation.

I could go on for pages describing the misuse of NPS involvement, but I think I've made my point. Members of Congress are not bad people—they are doing exactly what the people who elected them want them to do. And their projects aren't bad as promoters of economic development and tourism. But I seriously question whether these and other projects are legitimate undertakings for the Park Service.

While I was director, I searched for a way to recognize local or regional areas of interest without bringing them into the national park system. Mayors and hard-working civic leaders who would come to my office to petition us for help weren't always sure what they wanted beyond some sort of recognition. Some wanted their site taken into the park system because they could no longer afford to take care of it, while others just wanted a pat on the back and some sign of official designation that would raise their community's stature. These people were always dedicated and well meaning, but some seemed to think that our pockets were overflowing and that we could easily spare a few hundred thousand to launch their projects. They would become vague when asked about the annual operating budgets for those projects in the years ahead.

As I mentioned before, Associate Director Deny Galvin and I conceived the American Heritage Areas concept as a way of allowing the NPS to formally recognize a project, to provide some initial planning and funding assistance, but without becoming permanently involved. The idea of local interest groups working in partnership with the federal government and others to set aside and protect worthy areas is the wave of the future. But if future administrations and Congress don't tackle this problem before the blood of the NPS becomes too thin, our existing natural and cultural treasures that are part of the national park system will suffer irreparably.

With all my complaints about Congress, I was fortunate to have some good relationships with people there during my four years. Congressman Sid Yates of Illinois was chairman of the House Subcommittee on

Interior Appropriations. He was a very important man for me to get to know, as he held power over the Park Service budget. I had heard him described as a tough old bird, frosty and difficult to get along with. I spent nights doing my homework to know as much as possible about the NPS budget I was to present to him and members of his subcommittee. I walked into that first hearing with hundreds of details swirling around in my head and a healthy dose of anxiety about the hours ahead.

A Trip Down the New River in West Virginia
Ann Ridenour, Matt Ridenour, his wife Andrea, Jim Ridenour
and New River Gorge Superintendent Joe Kennedy, plus an
unidentified oarsman.

As it turned out, I liked Sid Yates. His style of questioning made me think of Groucho Marx on the old "You Bet Your Life" show. He asked one question after another, rarely giving me a chance for a full response.

Often the questions didn't seem to relate to one another. I'd heard he had been a prosecuting attorney early in his career. I'll bet he was a good one.

An apparent blunder on my part in that first hearing turned out to be one of the best political moves I made in dealing with the Congress. To understand what happened, I have to explain the fundamental steps in the budgeting process.

As NPS director, I was responsible for preparing a budget request that would be reviewed and modified by the secretary of the Interior. From the secretary's office the request went to the Office of Management and Budget (OMB), the budget people for the president, for further review. As a bureau director, I wasn't supposed to tell the OMB staff about my original request but was expected to support the figures that the secretary had approved and had made part of the Interior Department budget.

From those figures, the OMB created the president's budget. As you might surmise, I was now to forget the request of the secretary as well as my original request and support the numbers in the president's budget. Let me tell you, this is one confusing process.

The game continues when you reach Congress. With an eye toward making the executive branch look bad, the committee chairman always wants to know why you haven't asked for more money. After all, the papers are full of the problems of the parks—lack of maintenance, inadequate employee housing.... As expected, Chairman Yates asked me why I wasn't asking for more money. He spent a long time pointing out various deficiencies he had been reading about in the parks. I continued to support the president's budget.

Then Mr. Yates caught me by surprise by asking if I would allow the regional directors to send him a list of their actual needs—not the pared-down version in the budget request. He wanted a list that was unscrubbed by all the middlemen. For a moment I hesitated. I would most certainly be setting up a confrontational situation if I declined his request, and he would surely reap headlines over our failure to request funds to take care of the parks. On the other hand, I would be breaking the silent code of ethics of the executive branch if I allowed him to see anything other than the president's budget.

My answer was yes, and I directed the regional directors to comply with the chairman's request. It was the best move I ever made as far as the budget goes. When Chairman Yates saw the size of the requests that came in from the regional directors, he knew there wasn't enough money in the bank to take care of all those needs, and he couldn't beat up on Jim Ridenour and the NPS for failing to tell him about them. Effectively, we had put the ball in his court. He didn't ask for the full story at the next year's budget hearing. He knew and I knew that there wasn't enough money lying around not earmarked for other agencies to take care of the total needs of the Park Service.

On the Senate side I often dealt with Dale Bumpers, who chaired our authorizing subcommittee and served on our appropriations subcommittee. Senator Bumpers has a sense of humor and uses it frequently in his hearings. He has a great interest in the parks, especially the Civil War battlefields. Somehow, most hearings he held turned to talk of the Civil War. In Indiana we study the Civil War and have Civil War-buff clubs, but it wasn't until I moved to Virginia that the Civil War became a daily topic of discussion for me.

When Senator Bumpers would tire of questioning us about the matter at hand, the Civil War questions started to flow. I would soon exhaust my knowledge of certain generals and the intricacies of their troop movements. When the senator could see I was stuck and groping for answers, he would graciously let me off the hook by asking, "Jim, did you bring Ed Bearss with you? Ed knows where every man got shot, where he fell, and what caliber bullet got him." The senator was right. Ed is the chief historian of the NPS and has the most remarkable memory for detail of any man I've ever met. Ed often leads Civil War battlefield tours for the Smithsonian and other groups. If you ever get a chance to take a tour with Ed, don't miss it.

If I had to name one congressman who devoted more of his time to park matters than anyone else, it would be Bruce Vento of Minnesota. He chairs the authorizing subcommittee that deals with park issues in the House.

Many times when you deal with congressional committees you feel as if the members are getting prepared as the hearings are taking place. Sometimes they read from lists of questions that have obviously been prepared by staff. Sometimes staffers whisper questions into the members' ears. Some never ask or say anything.

Not Congressman Vento. He had a lot to say and was well prepared to say it. I believe he has a genuine interest in the parks, and there were a great many issues we agreed on. During the four years I was in Washington I would like to think I convinced Chairman Vento that our greatest problem was the creation of too many parks that were not truly of national stature.

A new idea for the creation of a park had to go through his subcommittee, and they slipped through much less easily at the end of my four years than at the beginning. To the chairman's credit, he could see we were starving our park system with an overpopulation of parks. Since parks don't generally have predators, the more marginal ones we create, the thinner the blood of the system becomes. By saying there are no predators I am saying that we rarely decommission a park once it is created. We probably won't see that happen unless something like a military-base-closure commission is established to review the parks. There is no doubt in my mind that a number of parks we have now should not be in the national park system, but closing any of them is very tough politically.

Like Chairman Yates, Chairman Vento had an interesting way of questioning a witness. I was told that he would make rather long, sometimes rambling statements, and somewhere in the statement would be a question. I was warned to listen carefully to pick it up and remember it. When a committee member is making a long statement it is often for the press and the people back home and may not have much to do with the subject at hand. As a witness it is tempting to be organizing your thoughts rather than paying close attention to the committee member. You couldn't get by doing that with Mr. Vento. Seemingly out of nowhere would come a question. When he said, "Wouldn't you agree with that, Mr. Director?" you'd better have listened to what he said. All these hearings are carefully recorded, and you can be made to look pretty stupid agreeing with a position that you had disagreed with an hour before.

Senator Bumpers and representatives Yates and Vento are all members of the majority party, which holds the committee chairmanships. But it would be a mistake to think the other party is asleep at the wheel. Particularly active were people like Ralph Regula of Ohio, Joe McDade of Pennsylvania, Bob Lagomarsino of California, Jim Hansen of Utah, Craig Thomas of Wyoming, Senator Mark Hatfield of Oregon, Senator Malcolm Wallop of Wyoming and Senator Don Nickles of Oklahoma.

I did not spend as much time on Capitol Hill as I probably should have. Directors of the past such as George Hartzog were legends for their drive to work with members of Congress. About once a week I told myself to spend more time on the Hill, but I felt so strongly that the NPS needed to return to the executive branch that I preferred running my agency rather than spending a day roaming the halls of Congress. Besides, every time I went up there I came back with a long list of special favors that members wanted for their districts. I could have spent my whole time on special favors, which seemed counterproductive to the big picture of the NPS.

It was clear to me that the Park Service needed to be brought back within the executive branch. We needed to do something or we were going to drown in a shower of congressionally mandated spending. Our traditional parks were shabby, our employees were poorly paid and housed. We needed money but we needed it in the right places.

I had this theory that the members of Congress, particularly those who followed the Park Service closely, had a budget figure in mind before we ever put in a request. My thought was that they took last year's budget and multiplied it by 105 percent or some such number, and that was going to be our budget no matter what we asked for. I often thought of the millions of dollars spent on preparing the budget—the thousands of hours in hearings, the months upon months of haggling over the darn thing. We could just use the old multiplier principle and have it over in five minutes! If you wanted to raise it, just pick a multiplier like 105 percent. If you wanted to cut it, you could pick a multiplier like 94 percent. I doubt that anyone will pick up on this theory of budgeting as it is too easy and thousands of government numbers crunchers would lose their jobs.

My plan was to increase the administration's request with worthy programs and projects—things we actually needed—in an attempt to shrink that vast area of congressional playground. If Congress already had a number in mind for us, I would try to get as close to that number with worthwhile spending and leave as little room for pork as possible.

In my final two years I succeeded. For the first time in anyone's memory, Congress actually cut our operations request. This was our bread-and-butter account—the money we needed to operate the parks. In 1993, they actually cut our operating budget by $47 million plus; they added on more than $90 million worth of construction funds we didn't ask for. To be fair to Congress, at least the stuff they added was somewhere on our list of things to do, but it wasn't high priority. (See Table 8.1.)

In the following table, ONPS is the operating account for the NPS. All the monies needed to operate the parks on a daily basis are included in this account. HPF is the Historic Preservation Fund account and includes the money to administer the national register program and some grant funds. Construction is the money allocated to construction projects. Land refers to money to purchase land and JFK refers to money needed to run the Kennedy Center in Washington, D.C.

The cut in the operations budget was real. We had no option other than to plan how we would cope with the cuts. I asked the regional directors to propose what they would have to do in their parks. I wanted each park to have maximum flexibility in making the decision, but I wanted to make sure the regional directors didn't let some superintendents go off the deep end.

When the stories began hitting the newspapers, my telephone started ringing off the hook. "You can't shut down the road in Shenandoah— it's in my district!" "You have to have rangers in the back country or people will get lost!" The lamenting went on and on.

I took care to point out to each caller that Congress had cut the president's operations budget request in order to add things we didn't ask for. To the members of Congress I called, I pointed out that they were strangling us for operating money while overloading us with capital projects we hadn't requested. Many of them acknowledged the problem and promised to look more carefully the next time, but in the meantime, "Don't cut anything in my district!"

It was the first good sign that we were on our way to becoming an executive branch agency again. We'd been working slowly to regain our status by actually proposing some legislation rather than just reacting. Now we were gaining some control over our budget. Hallelujah! (Table 8.1 next page).

Table 8.1/Difference between administration requests and Congressional action, fiscal years 1990 through 1993. ($ in thousands).

	ADMINISTRATIVE REQUEST	ENACTED	DIFFERENCE
	1990		
ONPS	740,370	776,804	+27,434
NR&P	10,204	15,923	+5,719
HPF	0	32,308	+32,308
CONST	44,112	197,407	+153,295
LAND	15,779	87,502	+71,723
JFK	15,193	9,118	-6,075
TOTAL	825,288	1,110,062	+284,404
	1991		
ONPS	821,805	867,688	+54,883
NR&P	10,125	18,301	+8,176
HPF	33,665	34,483	+818
CONST	83,659	270,443	+186,784
LAND	71,001	136,791	+65,790
JFK	8,150	21,039	+12,889
TOTAL	1,028,405	1,357,745	329,340
	1992		
ONPS	970,526	953,498	-17,028
NR&P	28,949	21,812	-7,137
HPF	35,931	35,478	-453
CONST	115,896	271,181	+155,285
LAND	117,645	105,227	-12,418
JFK	22,945	22,656	-289
TOTAL	1,291,892	1,409,852	117,960
	1993		
ONPS	1,031,813	983,995	-47,818
NR&P	30,991	23,563	-7,428
HPF	40,931	36,617	-4,314
CONST	137,686	229,831	+92,145
LAND	144,404	117,900	-26,504
JFK	13,556	20,629	+7,073
TOTAL	1,399,381	1,412,535	+13,154

9

Boondoggle in North Carolina

There are so many boondoggles it is unfair to pick out one for illustration—but I will anyway. This is about a place called Oregon Inlet on the outer banks of North Carolina.

First, I want to say that North Carolina is one of my favorite places in the world. My wife and I have often talked about owning a home in North Carolina someday. That state has a little bit of everything going for it from the mountains on the west to the beautiful shoreline on the east. God was good to North Carolina.

Oregon Inlet is just what it says—a passageway through the dune shoreline into the Wanchese Bay. In 1978 the state, in conjunction with the federal government, put approximately $8 million into building a small fisheries industry in the bay. There are six fisheries processing plants that service about eighteen boats stationed in the harbor that are primarily fishing for bluefins, trout and flounder. Altogether the industry provides somewhere in the neighborhood of twenty-five to two hundred jobs, fluctuating by season.

The problem is that the channel into Oregon Inlet is constantly filling with sand and is shifting location. This is not something new; there has always been fairly large-scale shifting of sand and beach erosion along the coast. Openings to the calmer water of the bay have come and gone over the years and will continue to do so despite the feeble efforts of man to overcome the natural world.

For years, going back as far as the early 1960s, politicians of North Carolina have tried to get some form of construction that would block the sand from filling in the entrance to the bay. Oregon Inlet has been kept open all these years by dredging, but some of the locals would like to see some massive structure that they think would solve their problems.

The Park Service owns much of the land on the north side of the inlet and U.S. Fish and Wildlife owns much of the barrier island to the south. This whole area has been a moving, shifting dune area long before there was ever a Park Service or a fishing fleet.

The U.S. Army Corps of Engineers, the very same agency that gave us the water plumbing system that has messed up South Florida, has been encouraged by powerful North Carolina interests to think of mechanical ways to disrupt the natural flow of sand along the shore in an attempt to keep Oregon Inlet open.

I have to say that the corps is finally beginning to notice that the answer to every problem does not automatically involve the pouring of concrete. My experience as chairman of the Great Lakes Commission during the high waters of the mid-1980s taught me that hardening shorelines to protect homes that should never have been there in the first place puts enormous burdens on the taxpayer and rarely accomplishes the intended protection. If anything, the big concrete *solution* causes more problems than it solves.

The drift of sand in that area is predominantly north to south. If you stick two long arms of concrete out to sea in an attempt to disrupt the drift it doesn't take an engineer to figure out that sand will pile up on the north side of the arm or jetty, as it is called, and the shore to the south of the arm will get "sand starved."

You can count on this—it is not speculation. If you want to see a good example of where this is occurring, all you have to do is get an overhead view of the south end of Ocean City, Maryland, and notice what it has done and continues to do to Assateague Island. Ocean City has trapped sand on the north and Assateague is slowly starving to the south. This is what would happen at Oregon Inlet.

"But," say the engineers, "we will devise a magnificent system of pipes and pumps that will suck sand from the north, under the inlet and deposit it to the south. It might work.

"And, by the way, we will need to build the arms or jetties over one mile out to sea where they will need to be strong enough to stand the tremendous winter assaults that are famous on the Outer Banks."

So now we are talking about a system that might work—no assurances—and we haven't talked costs yet. For starters, construction costs alone are estimated to be in the $90 million range, and I have yet to see a project that didn't cost considerably more than the preliminary estimates. In addition there will need to be continual maintenance on the structure probably costing somewhere in the neighborhood of $8 million per year.

The bottom line is that the north shore will face disruption. The chances are better than fifty-fifty that the south shore or Pea Island will slowly disappear, and the taxpayer is going to foot a bill in excess of $100 million for construction and who knows how much for maintenance.

All of this to salvage what remains of a small coastal fishery that supplies approximately twenty fulltime jobs to the local economy in addition to the seasonal jobs with the fishing fleet.

You could give all job holders around $3 million each and tell them to have a good life or, if commercial fishing is their dying passion, they could take the money and invest in far better equipment and far better fishing areas in far better locations.

Now, I really don't think that Secretary Lujan ever intended to give the North Carolinians the permits to start this absurd logrolling but the governor of North Carolina was an old congressional friend of his and, of course, Senator Jesse Helms was anxious to keep this boondoggle alive and claimed that victory was just around the corner the whole year of the election.

There were serious legal doubts that the secretary had the authority to grant any kind of permit for this project. The essence of the legal argument was that you would have to give up parkland and fish and wildlife land to make this thing work and some thought that only Congress could make that decision.

With all the people lined up to sue, I am sure the case would have gone to court and there it would have remained for a considerable length of time.

I don't want to leave the impression that this whole show was a Republican boondoggle in the making. With the change in administration and the election of a Democrat governor in North Carolina, I see from newspaper accounts that North Carolina is again pushing the secretary of Interior to support this project. The account I read was that the secretary would look into it.

Secretaries have been "looking into" this project since Rogers Morton in the 1960s. It has never made sense and it isn't getting better. As far as the Corps of Engineers taming the movements of the sea—fat chance. Keep an eye on this one.

10

Interest Groups—In Whose Interest?

During my years in Washington I was bombarded by interest groups. Some were serious and well spoken. Others were off the wall and they knew it. With some it was a game—a way to blow off steam and have a good time. With others the stakes were high and the discussions intense.

On my first trip to Yellowstone I was invited to an all-employee picnic. I had my wife along and the park officials had planned a very nice carry-in dinner. It had the old-time feeling of a large family reunion in the park. After a long day of travel, I was prepared for a relaxing evening.

I knew that Earth First! was active in the park and was a big supporter of wolf reintroduction, but I wasn't prepared to see people skipping through the lawn areas of Mammoth Hot Springs with all kinds of animal costumes on. They were carrying protest signs of one kind or another and seemed to be having a great time. They were obviously trying to attract attention to themselves and were hopeful that the media might be covering my arrival at the park.

This particular group has irritated the rangers to no end from time to time and I could tell that feelings between the law enforcement rangers and this group were tense. In the past this group has organized demonstrations, even chained themselves to trees or other key locations in the park to attract attention to one concern or another. I am sure they can be a nuisance but on the day of my visit they looked more like a fun-loving group of mischief makers from the streets of Berkeley in the 1960s.

The park officials anticipated trouble but had given Earth First! a permit to demonstrate in a certain area, although they were not to invade the area where the picnic was to take place. When it came time for the picnic, I noticed that the demonstrators had come as close to the picnic grounds as their permit would allow and were shouting and waving signs. The rangers were clearly disgusted to have this group spoil the first visit of the boss.

Maybe it is my Hoosier roots that has forged my management style, but I have always believed in trying to talk with people in an attempt to try to understand what their concerns are. When I mentioned to the superintendent that I thought I would walk over and talk with the demonstrators, he was not at all thrilled with the idea and thought that little good could come from it. I decided to give it a try anyway. As I walked toward this wildly decorated, sign-waving, noisy crew I began to wonder if I had made the right decision. Some of them had a pretty tough reputation and were not beyond the destruction of government property to get their point across. I was definitely government property.

I zeroed in on a small section of people who appeared to be in a leadership position. I asked them to calm down so I could speak to them. They were so shocked that I came over that they actually calmed down. I noticed rangers scattered about in positions ready to take action if action were needed. It kind of felt like one of the old shoot-out scenes in the western movies.

My request was simple, "Look, my family and I are trying to get to know the Yellowstone people in a family-style picnic. You are disrupting what would otherwise be a very enjoyable evening for us. I am willing to sit down and talk with you as long as you want to talk, but I want you to respect my right to privacy tonight. I will meet with you right here in the picnic grounds tomorrow over a cup of coffee and we can talk all you want."

I had no idea what the response would be and the Earth First! people were looking at each other as if to say, "Is this guy for real? Will he keep this promise?" After milling around and mumbling to each other they decided to take me up on the deal. They went away peaceably. Of course, that got the attention of the rangers. They were sure I must have promised to give away the park in order to make peace with the Earth First! people.

The morning meeting with Earth First! went fine. They had their chance to be heard and seemed to be appreciative. They knew some of their demands were on the far side of ridiculous and, at times, they almost broke into a grin when presenting one wild idea or another, but they did get their chance to be heard and that was what they wanted.

Speaking of interest groups, when I was first appointed I noticed I was getting dinged in the press by the Sierra Club. They were trying to make me out as some sort of a development-minded zealot who would put a golf course in every park. I was curious as to why they were attacking me as I had always gotten along with the Indiana chapter of the Sierra Club. In fact, many of the Indiana chapter members called me to say that this bad-mouthing was not coming from them and they would write the national chapter to try to get this media garbage stopped.

As time went on I realized that the Sierra Club was looking for someone or something to attack in order to keep those membership dollars rolling in. All special interest groups have to have an enemy or they have a tough time raising the money to pay salaries.

By chance, I was in San Francisco and met the executive director of the Sierra Club in a social setting. He warmly greeted me and told me how much they were looking forward to working with me. I asked him why they were trashing me in the press if they were so excited about working with me. He smiled sheepishly and tried to change the subject. I couldn't help but stick in a little barb. "I know James Watt turned out to be one of your greatest fund-raisers, and I want you to know that I do not intend to provide you with the ammunition to raise money that he did." From that time on my relationship with the Sierra Club went pretty well. We didn't always agree but we were not nasty to each other. We were actually in concert on a number of important issues.

The National Parks and Conservation Association is a citizens' advocate group for parks. They have over 400,000 members and are quite active on The Hill and in various regions of the country. I actively worked with the NPCA, although there were times when what the NPS was trying to accomplish and what the NPCA wanted was in conflict. As in most public interest groups, NPCA had staffers that occasionally went beyond common sense in pushing one cause or another. Sometimes that worked to my advantage as I could be seen as the voice of logic striving for the reasonable position that Congress was searching for as opposed to the more strident position NPCA was taking on an issue. Paul Pritchard, the president of NPCA, and I understood this sometimes contentious relationship well and worked it to the advantage of the parks on a number of occasions.

On the ultraconservative side of public interest groups, one name comes to mind: Chuck Cushman of the National Association of In Holders. The In Holders are an association of people who own land within the boundaries of a federal area and have banded together under the very capable leadership of Chuck Cushman to fight all kinds of federal threats—real or imagined. (Chuck is in the process of changing the name of his group to the American Land Rights Association. Too many people thought the old name made them sound like hotel owners in the parks.)

To say Chuck is generally disliked by NPS personnel is an understatement. Many see Chuck as a chief despoiler of the environment and a leader in thwarting the protection of many of the resources for which the parks were created.

I have had Chuck come to Indiana University to lecture my public-policy classes. My message is that Chuck and people like Chuck are out there and they are extremely effective. Chuck himself is an excellent lecturer and a very pleasant fellow in a social situation, but he is a high-powered opponent and can wreak havoc in the most innocent of governmental programs if he takes a notion.

Chuck sometimes bills himself as "rent a riot." He tells me that he has eight fax machines and over fourteen thousand fax numbers scattered across the United States. He claims to be able to cause anything from a near riot to a peaceful demonstration once he decides to turn the fax machines loose. I believe him. He did it to us on a simple little program dealing with the designation of national natural landmarks.

The idea of having a national natural landmarks program grew out of the movement of having a program of national historic landmarks. Where is our tallest mountain? What is our deepest cave? What is our longest river? Where is the habitat of one endangered species or another?

In many cases, people would write us and urge that we investigate something unique on their land in the hope that they would gain landmark status. Often these would be people who were hoping to capitalize on the fact that they had something for a tourist to see and that it was worthy of national status.

Chuck Cushman became convinced that we were designating these areas with the intent of taking them away from the owners to create new national park sites. As far as I was concerned, we couldn't pay for the park sites we already had, and the national natural landmarks program was a good way to instill pride and an interest in having landowners protect the sites without government ownership or management.

Chuck cranked up his fax machines and it wasn't long before the secretary of Interior and many members of Congress wondered what in the hell we were doing to incite all of these citizens. I have to admit that this program was rather low priority and had not been run very efficiently or with a lot of oversight. I jumped in with both feet to save a rather innocuous program that had merit but was floundering under Chuck Cushman's weight, which is considerable.

I soon found out that Chuck had close ties within the NPS that were feeding him stories to use against us. I also found that he had ingenious ways to make mail appear from everywhere. He had those fax machines working by zip code around the clock.

Some of our own so-called friends didn't help as they rushed to discount what Chuck had to say. Chuck loves publicity, positive or negative—he thrives on it. He can't stand being ignored. So the great war of the fax machines continues today. The national natural landmarks program is on hold while someone investigates whether or not it is some sort of a Communist plot, and Chuck is moving on to other things such as the spotted owl and timber grazing and mining rights.

It is safe to say that I don't discount Chuck Cushman. He makes a living proving what one man can do with a copier and a fax.

Of course, there are interest groups to fit every occasion. Sometimes they are sincere, and sometimes they are a thinly disguised attempt to take money out of your pocket and put it in theirs. I became very suspicious of groups that purported to represent the parks—especially when none or very little of their revenues ever reached a park.

It is important that we have these widely divergent opinions and discussions on issues of national importance. I listened to some pretty crazy stuff during my tenure and some members of my staff probably thought I was overly patient with some of the off-the-wall groups. In my way of looking at it, if I only listened to people who thought like me, I would never have a new thought. It is easy to become isolated in a top job in government or private industry. That is why it is so important to get outside the beltway to find out what is going on in the country if you are going to be an effective leader.

11

The Deteriorating Infrastructure of Our Parks

One of my biggest surprises was to discover what poor condition many of our national parks are in. Roads, trails, employee housing, buildings, sewer systems and other infrastructure are in bad shape without a great deal of hope for a quick fix.

There is a lot of debate over just how big the backlog of critical maintenance projects is, but a conservative estimate would value it in the neighborhood of at least $2 billion. The infrastructure of the national park system is sliding into mediocrity. Congress is quick to give the Park Service new construction projects but loathe to give it the people and the money to take care of its facilities once they are built. Table 8.1 will give you an example of what I mean. The most important category of funds for those who operate the parks is the operations account called ONPS. This account pays for operations and maintenance including the salaries of full-time and seasonal rangers and the maintenance staff.

In 1992, for the first time in recent memory, the Congress failed to give the NPS the relatively bare-bones operating budget it requested. But note that it gave us more than $150 million above what we asked for in construction funds. The 1993 budget was even worse. Congress cut our operations budget by over $47 million and stuck in an extra $92 million in construction. The old construction park barrel didn't slow down even with the NPS in desperate need for operating monies. I had no choice but to cut back on programs and people. In some cases that meant shutting down facilities completely or at least for a period of time. My instructions were to make the cuts where they would have the least impact on the visiting public.

Members of Congress and their staffs went bananas when they found out that things were being cut back or closed in their districts. I reminded them of the growing impacts that "park barreling" was having on us and that they couldn't expect us to keep the parks operational if all the money was pouring into construction projects—most of which we didn't need or want or were low priority.

My first trip to Grand Canyon National Park was a real eye-opener in many ways. There was the canyon and it certainly is grand. But if you can tear your eyes away from that beautiful sight and look around with some intensity, you will find Park Service employees living in miserable conditions, repair shops desperately in need of repair, and the overall man-made environment subpar or worse.

The same can be said for almost any of the parks. The government has just not taken care of these beautiful treasures.

At Independence National Historical Park, Independence Hall itself is in bad repair and needs major infrastructure work. The problem is that the kind of work it needs is not where people will see it. It is plumbing and wiring and things like that. These types of renovation are expensive to fix and they don't lend themselves to dedication events and ribbon cuttings. So they languish on the priority list as Congress looks for more "sexy" projects.

Sequoia National Park is another area that has major infrastructure problems. The old system has just worn out. On a visit to Sequoia I turned into the parking lot to register for a room at the inn. I noticed water running down the pavement and, upon closer look, I noticed toilet paper. The old sewer system was overloaded and the pipes were clogged up. I couldn't believe it—here we were trying to set the environmental standard for the nation and we were in blatant violation of the standards ourselves. Superintendent Tom Ritter was working as hard as he could to straighten up the mess but had neither the money nor the manpower to get the job done.

One of my early inspections took me to the Kennedy Center in Washington, D.C. I had been surprised to learn that the Park Service had the responsibility for maintaining the building and its public areas. I found the place in terrible shape. The roof leaked, the sidewalks were cracked, the carpet needed replacing, the mechanical systems were nearly worn out, and the levels of underground parking were in various stages of decay. I couldn't believe it! I'm not an engineer, but it didn't take a genius to figure out that the place was falling apart. Something had to be done. Why hadn't this been reported before? Or, if it had, why hadn't something been done about it?

The production side of the Kennedy Center budget was not a Park Service responsibility, but everything that took place outside the individual theater doors was. There were so many things that needed doing in the parks, and I was very reluctant to start pouring millions of dollars into fixing up what was obviously a very poorly constructed facility. I sensed that the big dollars that would be needed for the Kennedy Center would come out of the hide of the parks that desperately needed attention. I was right. But I was even more determined that I would not stick my head in the sand and ignore the problem. I would not let that building fall down on my watch.

At the first meeting of the Kennedy Center's board of trustees I attended, I pledged my support to work to solve the problems of the building. There was a great deal of talk about how much money the center was losing and how the deficit was not being made up by donations. I heard this great, booming voice speaking out against the growing deficit and calling for restraint in spending. I thought I recognized the owner of that voice and looked across the room to spy Senator Ted Kennedy. With my conservative midwestern background I couldn't believe it—a Kennedy speaking out for spending restraints and deficit reduction! In the following four years I found Senator Kennedy a voice of reason on the board and appreciated his care and concern. I learned that the public man and the private man aren't always one and the same.

As for that booming voice: Senator Kennedy must have been thirty feet away but he sounded as if he were right beside me. How had he projected so well? Part of the answer, I discovered, lay in the beautiful concave ceiling over the area where the board usually meets. It has the effect of reflecting conversations from one part of the room to the other—even whispers can be clearly heard.

This brought many amusing moments in what were sometimes dull meetings. One of our attendees fell asleep as the afternoon wore on. We had enjoyed a large lunch that he was having apparent difficulty digesting. The unmistakable sound of breaking wind echoed like thunder all around the room as people of high fashion and good breeding did their best to politely ignore the gentleman. I wanted to do this friend a favor and wake him up, but doing so would call increased attention to him, so on he slept. Poor fellow! He will probably never know that he was providing moments of mirth while the unending reports were being given. Unless he reads this chapter.

Jim Wohlfenson, president and chairman of the board, Kennedy Center; Jim Ridenour, director, NPS.
Jim Wohlfenson was never happy that the Kennedy Center budget came through the National Park Service. Here he tells me of another in a long line of emergencies requiring increased appropriations for the Center. Unfortunately, he was right. He and I agreed that the building was falling apart. The Center was a good example of Congress spending big dollars for new construction and then failing to support the ongoing operation.

On another occasion, a relatively new member of the board was whispering to her neighbor about her unhappiness that other members of the board didn't give as much to the Kennedy Center as she did. There was some talk that board members should give, or at least raise, $100,000 for the center in exchange for the privilege of their appointment. (I hoped they didn't expect that much from me, an ex officio member, on civil servant's wages!) The new member's tongue was sharp and her whispers reached every ear in the room. All the others must have been mentally totaling up their contributions as she complained, "I'll bet some of them even charge expenses to come to the board meetings!"

Grand Canyon, Independence, Sequoia and the Kennedy Center are not isolated examples of deterioration in the parks. Such problems are commonplace all over the park system. This is why I would get so angry when Congress would assign us another pork park project and ignore our real problems.

President Bush, Secretary Lujan and a few members of Congress understood the situation, and we did launch a program to eliminate the maintenance backlog by 1999. Of course, we left office in 1993, so we will have to see how it turns out.

We had a hard time getting the Congress to go along with our increased requests for maintenance funds. If I had had the money they assigned to park barrel projects I could have put a dent in many of those serious problems, but it is hard to get the Congress to think in terms of stewardship and maintenance. I guess when you are elected for two-year terms you think in two-year cycles. The statesmen with an understanding of the longer term were few and far between.

12

Money—We Always Need Money

A big disappointment I had on my first national park inspection tour was with the woeful state of the man-made environment inside the parks. Earlier I mentioned my eye-opening experience at Grand Canyon National Park, where I found employees living and working in conditions that would not meet the standards of my home state park system in Indiana.

Grand Canyon isn't an exception; it's the rule. Almost every park I visited suffered from a lack of maintenance. The superintendents are struggling to keep the gates open from an operational standpoint while holding the physical plant together with baling wire and bubble gum.

Most people thought I went to the parks to enjoy the great vistas, and I did my share of that, but the primary purpose for many visits was to look at deteriorating infrastructure. I saw more malfunctioning sewer systems and potholes than I hope to see the rest of my life.

To be fair, I imagine that a tour of much of the country would reveal the same conditions. The infrastructure we proudly built in the 1950s and 1960s is now starting to crumble, and we don't have the money to fix it. Roads that were gravel when I was a young kid growing up in Indiana were paved when I was a teenager. Now when I go home for a visit, the potholes have grown so big that the county commissioners have made the roads gravel again. Let's face it, as a country we're getting older—and not very gracefully.

The maddening thing is that the Park Service was never hurting for new project money—at least money for new projects in the states of influential members of the appropriations committees in Congress. We couldn't build things as fast as the new money poured in. We just never were given enough money to take care of what we already had.

True to his rhetoric, President Reagan tried to hold down spending and the deficit and never asked for adequate money to take care of the park system. Pay close attention. Notice I said President Reagan didn't *ask* for much money for the parks. That doesn't mean he didn't get a lot. In 1987, for example, he asked for approximately $30 million for new construction in the parks. The Congress gave him more than $88 million. In that same year, the president's request for land acquisition was $13 million and Congress appropriated $75 million.

The march to the trough was picking up steam. It really got out of hand in President Reagan's last budget submission for the 1989 fiscal year. The president asked for $15 million in new construction for the parks. The Congress gave him $159 million. Even if you believe Congress was trying to do the right thing by the parks, you can't justify that wide a discrepancy in terms other than pork barrel, or as I can't help calling it again, park barrel. You might think the Park Service would welcome all that extra money, but most of it was earmarked for congressmen's pet projects and couldn't be used for things the parks needed most.

So President Reagan got more money than he asked for, didn't hold down the federal deficit, and put the parks in worse operating condition than before. The Congress loaded him up with more questionable parks to take care of but didn't give him the operational funds to do the job. I don't want to single out President Reagan; this same sort of thing went on during the terms of many presidents. Until a president gets some sort of line-item authority over the congressional budget process, there will never be a balanced budget. The Congress hangs bells and whistles all over appropriations bills, knowing the president must act on entire bills and is seldom able to veto them.

Even if the president gets a line-item veto so he can nix tax-wasting items in an appropriations bill, members of Congress will load the bill with goodies for the folks back home and then cry, "I tried my best but the president vetoed that new park or project I worked for in our district."

The process of putting an appropriations bill together is a great mystery. It doesn't follow any of the textbook theories that are taught in our

114

universities. As nearly as I can tell, Congress thinks incrementally. The appropriations committees take last year's figures as a starting point, then add on a little for the next year. In other words, they know about what the budget for the Park Service is going to be before anyone has taken the time to learn what is needed. What a waste of time! Hundreds of hours of overtime and millions of dollars are spent putting together the president's budget request, and then Congress largely ignores all but the most highly featured items in it. Those areas where Congress largely ignores the executive submission are where you will find the most congressional pork—in construction and lands acquisition budgets.

I decided it would be interesting to compare what the NPS requested for construction and land acquisition to what they actually got from Congress from 1983 to 1993. The following table is the result of that comparison. The NPS got well over $1 billion more than requested during this period. Most agencies wouldn't complain if they got more than they asked for, but the problem was that Congress didn't direct the money to areas where we needed it. To be fair to Congress, some of this money went to projects that the NPS wanted but were too low on the priority list to make the budget request, but much of it was pure pork barrel and *oinked* on the way to being spent (See *Table 12-1*)

We could save tons of money if Congress would just say, "This year we have a little extra money so, NPS, you get 4 percent more. Or this year you get 6 percent less." We wouldn't have these horrendous budget fights that sap the body politic every year, and the results wouldn't be much different. We could cut employment significantly in both the executive and legislative branches. We would probably have to allow the president or the Congress to have one or two major policy changes per year that would impact the budget. Both branches could concentrate their energies on those issues and, hopefully, come closer to inventing good government packages rather than political mishmash.

The bottom line for parks is that there's never enough money to take care of their needs. People have different ideas about the Park Service's backlog of maintenance items, although I heard the figure $2 billion used rather routinely. I guarantee the Park Service couldn't wisely spend $2 billion in any short order. If it could, there would still be a $2 billion backlog. The park superintendents would find more things that needed fixing while they were fixing the major items included in the original backlog.

I'm not criticizing the superintendents; it's the nature of the problem they face. The problem is that government doesn't take care of things on a routine basis. It awaits a crisis before responding. You may recall my mentioning this kind of behavior when discussing the Kennedy Center.

If there's a solution that makes sense in the mad scramble for park funding, it may be a user-related excise tax. The fish and wildlife interests have done pretty well with this concept under a series of laws named for their congressional sponsors: Pittman-Robertson, Dingell-Johnson, and now Wallop-Breaux. Or as Senator John Breaux calls it, Breaux-Wallop. Senator Breaux told me he never wanted his name enshrined in a tax, but the wildlife conservation and management program it supports is very popular.

Revenues from these taxes on fishing and hunting gear and motorboat fuels used by hunters and fishermen go into a dedicated fund that is restricted to improving wildlife habitat in this country and increasing the safe hunting and boating skills of our citizens. I've rarely heard these taxes criticized. This is because those paying the fees know the money is coming back directly to benefit the improvement of wildlife habitat. They know that neither the executive nor the legislative branch can divert the income to other uses. This is absolutely key to the public acceptance of these taxes.

The same kind of funding mechanism could be used for the parks. For years there has been talk of instituting a similar user excise tax on outdoor recreation products. It makes sense. Without publicly provided lands, people couldn't find places to use many of these products. There are private campgrounds, to be sure, but even their patrons are often drawn by nearby parks or other significant features in the public domain.

Appropriations Requested Versus Enacted
$ In Thousands
Fiscal Years 1983 Through 1993

FISCAL YEAR	AMOUNT REQUESTED BY NPS	ENACTED BY CONGRESS	DIFFERENCE
CONSTRUCTION			
1983	132,721	159,096	+26.375
1984	78,275	66,690	-11,585
1985	77,878	111,045	+33,167
1986	49,456	112,408	+62,952
1987	29,114	88,095	+58,981
1988	30,798	93,017	+62,218
1989	15,003	159,108	+144,105
1990	44,112	197,407	+153,295
1991	83,659	270,443	+186,784
1992	115,896	271,181	+155,285
1993	137,686	229,831	+92,145
TOTAL	794,598	1,758,321	+963,723
LAND ACQUISITION			
1983	59,776	121,606	+61,830
1984	44,671	128,560	+83,979
1985	99.966	95,682	-4,284
1986	10,000	46,041	+36,041
1987	13,000	76,160	+62,160
1988	12,538	40,763	+28,225
1989	12,396	52,609	+40,213
1990	15,779	87,502	+71,723
1991	71,001	136,791	+65,790
1992	117,645	105,227	-12,418
1993	144,404	117,900	-26,504
TOTAL	601,176	1,007,931	+406,755
SUBTOTAL CONSTRUCTION	794,598	1,758,321	+963,723
SUBTOTAL LAND	601,176	1,007,931	+406,755
GRAND TOTAL	1,395,773	2,766,252	+1,370,478

Director Ridenour and Redwood National Park Superintendent Bill Ehorn study a map in the shadow of one of the giant
redwoods.

Kevin Kearney of the Naturist Society estimates that, in 1990, nearly
$18 billion was spent at the wholesale level for outdoor recreational
equipment. If you were to apply a 5 percent tax at the wholesale level
for this equipment and dedicate the revenue to providing outdoor recreational facilities, you would generate nearly $900 million. That's close
to the current operating budget of the entire National Park Service with
367 park sites, 80 million acres, and more than 14,000 employees.

118

In this vein, I'm struck by the tremendous rise in interest in slow-pitch softball. Everywhere I go I see people playing slow pitch. We played it in Washington, D.C., using the Washington Monument as a foul pole. There just aren't enough softball fields to accommodate the need. According to Kevin Kearney, approximately $270 million was spent on bats, balls, and gloves for this sport at the wholesale level in 1990. The 5 percent excise tax would yield more than $10 million for new playing fields across this country.

The list goes on and on. Think about putting a small percentage of bike sales into the tremendous demand for new biking trails across the country. Think about a percentage of hiking boot sales going into maintaining and expanding our hiking trails.

There are thorny issues to be worked out. For example, if you were to tax the sale of off-road recreational vehicles, how much of the revenue should go into public lands? Would it be fair to tax motor homes? If so, would you need to cap the tax per unit? These are details about which there is honest debate. But I'm convinced that parks and other public providers of outdoor recreation will remain underfunded until some sort of user-related excise tax program is put in place.

I see where the Clinton administration has proposed a significant increase in visitor and user fees for the parks. This is not a new idea; it came up in the Reagan years as well as during the Bush administration. I wanted to increase the fees to visit the parks, and I believed the American people would support the increase, but I wanted the increase only if at least half of it would remain in the parks and not go back to the general treasury to be controlled by the park barrel Congress.

If the Clinton plan is approved by Congress, the NPS would charge by the person rather than by the car as they have done in the past. For example, a car with five people in it would be charged $5 per person or $25 rather than the charge of $5 per car as it is now. There is speculation that this increase would bring in an additional $72 million by 1996. The parks need it.

I would be supportive of an increase if there were some guarantees that the Congress wouldn't cut the budget of the NPS using the excuse that the parks will generate their own money. I don't think it is realistic

119

to expect the parks to generate 100 percent of the revenue needed for operations funds from fees and charges.

Actually, there is at least one state, New Hampshire, that does take in enough money to run its park system. The state operates pretty lean and mean, and has the advantage of getting part of the revenues from ski areas within the parks, but it claims to operate the state parks on 100 percent generated revenues. My own state of Indiana used to figure that gate collections and other user fees would generate approximately 70 percent of the operating cost of the system. When I got to Washington and found that our national park sites were generating less than 10 percent of what was needed for operational funds I couldn't believe it.

We weren't charging enough and we weren't charging at all sites and, at the sites where we were charging, the collections were sporadic. If the superintendent needed the collections staff to work on something else, such as a forest fire, collections at the gate might be suspended. Who could blame the superintendents? They were often working shorthanded anyhow. They had to pay the gate attendants but the money they collected went to the general treasury. In other words, it cost the superintendent to collect and there was no incentive to work very hard at it. In fact, there was a disincentive.

In trying to come to a reasonable figure to collect, my theory has always been that the gate fees shouldn't be so high as to keep those who wanted to go from going because of the cost. The cost per person that the Clinton administration is considering may be a little high at five dollars per person. On the other hand, if you take your family to a movie anymore, you can rarely get by for less than five dollars per person. Somehow, charging five dollars for some of the trash put out by Hollywood seems almost sinful compared to taking your family to see the Grand Canyon.

Once people are inside the park, I believe they should pay their fair share for the use of facilities. For example, if a family is tent camping and trying to get by on a small budget, the fee for that kind of campsite should be very low. If someone pulls in with a huge motor home and wants hookups to electricity, water and sewer, the price should reflect those services. Actually, I would prefer that those kind of campsites should be outside the park whenever possible and, preferably, run by private operators.

My recommendation would be that Congress should get out of the fee-setting business. They should delegate that authority to the secretary of Interior so that fees are not set in the political arena of Congress. Many members of congress think of themselves as experts in fee setting but, more often than not, when they engage in a fee argument they are posturing for one special interest group or another. For example, one congressman from Florida didn't think his constituents ought to have to pay to visit the park site at Canaveral National Sea Shore since they lived in the area. Senator Bill Bradley objected to a one-dollar fee that was charged to visit the Statue of Liberty. We weren't getting complaints, but because of Senator Bradley's objection, we lost that income.

One of the toughest lobbying groups I dealt with at the state level was the one that represented senior citizens. The group was powerful and determined to see that senior citizens didn't have to pay increased fees. I know that seniors living on fixed incomes have a tough time, but most of the senior citizens who can afford to travel can afford the price to get into a park better than the poor guy with a family of four who just got laid off at the steel mill. In fact, our polls showed that seniors were more than willing to pay their fair share, but you couldn't convince the special-interest influence peddlers who represented the seniors to the state legislature of that point. They would get the bills assigned to committees that had marching orders to kill the bill. And the committees did so.

I doubt that the Congress will grant the Clinton administration the ability to administratively set fees in the parks. When it comes to money matters, the Congress very jealously guards what it believes to be its turf. A compromise might be that Congress could appoint a special commission that would consider fee-increase recommendations from the secretary of Interior and the secretary of Agriculture to cover both the parks and the forests. The commission could hold public hearings and have the final authority to make the decision. This would make more sense than trying to argue these issues in the halls of Congress.

A final point is that I think everyone should pay. There are so many good causes that I just don't see how you make the decision that one group pays and another doesn't. You could spend millions of dollars in time arguing that the disabled shouldn't have to pay but the Girl Scouts should. Or that veterans of World War II shouldn't but vets from the Korean conflict should. Or that Native Americans shouldn't. Believe me, I have had every kind of group apply for exempt status for paying that you could imagine. The list is endless. Better to have no exceptions— everyone pays is the best policy. With the cost of an annual pass kept at a reasonable level, I would probably even support having Park Service employees pay entrance fees, and you know darn well that I would support having members of Congress pay!

To cover the situations where groups truly cannot pay—for example, indigent children being bused to a park from the inner cities—a special fund made up of contributions from private industry or individuals could be established at each park site and used at the discretion of the superintendent. I don't think it would be hard to raise contributions to cover those situations and the "everyone pays" philosophy could stay intact.

This idea of the dedicated funds where at least half of the fees collected would stay in the park will have appeal to those paying the fee. They like to know that they are helping the park directly. Some say that it is just a plan that would make the rich parks richer—and there is some logic to the argument. What some congressional staff members are really saying is that the parks that are most popular will gain the most under a plan like this. What is wrong with that? The parks that people want to visit are the parks that need the money. Could it be that the parks that few want to visit are some of the park sites that came into the system as park barrel?

I don't want to appear overly cynical. There are important sites that would not benefit as well as others under the collection policy I have described. For example, Yellowstone, Grand Canyon and Yosemite would obviously benefit. The developing Alaskan parks might not. Nor would some of the less-visited cultural and historic sites. I believe that Congress and the administration could work these problems out, if and when they occur. What I do want to emphasize is that Congress should not and must not penalize a park for being heavily visited and efficient in its collection procedures. If a ranger can tell John Q. Public that the fee has gone up but the money is going to be used in the park to fix up the trails and hire more education staff, you will have a happy John Q. Public, in most instances.

Part Four

NPS & Concessionaires

13

Concessions at Your Service

When I was sworn in as director of the National Park Service, Interior Secretary Lujan had already decided that the NPS concessions regulations were badly in need of attention. I was told that the secretary was looking for reform and that the Park Service staff believed it was needed. I was also told that the quickest way to lose my recent appointment and be run out of town would be to cross swords with the park concessionaires. Another director had done so and was handed his walking papers.

In a meeting with the secretary to discuss the issues, I told him I'd heard that concessionaires could send you packing pretty quickly. He laughed. "I've been in town for quite a while, and if they send us home I can stand it," he said. "Mr. Secretary," I interjected, "I just arrived last week!"

True to the secretary's wishes we started on concessions reform immediately. While I was often given a royal roasting when I spoke to the concessionaires at their annual meetings amid hints that they might try to get me fired, I never felt any pressure from anyone other than the concessionaires themselves. I received constant encouragement and even prodding by Secretary Lujan to get on with the job of concessions reform.

At one of the annual meetings, Senator Malcolm Wallop of Wyoming spoke just before me. He gave a rousing speech about his support of the concessionaires and how they had a real friend in Malcolm Wallop. From his remarks you would have thought that the concessionaires had nothing to worry about. They gave him a standing ovation as he left the room.

Now it was my turn and I had to deliver the bad news. I was and am a fan of Senator Wallop, but I knew that everything wasn't rosy for the concessionaires. While they might have the support of Senator Wallop, there were other senators and members of Congress who sharply disagreed with his position. I felt it would be unfair to let them return home feeling that all was well for them in Washington. I gave them my observations of other attitudes around town and was soundly booed. I brought the message and they wanted to kill the messenger.

Their chairman, Rex Maughan, said that he personally was going to sue my socks off. I told him to give it his best effort. My lawyers weren't going to cost me anything, while his would be running up a big bill in a losing cause.

Later Senator Wallop asked me to his office for a visit. What I thought was going to be a pleasant meeting turned ugly quickly as the senator accused me of telling the concessionaires that his speech was all wrong and didn't represent the feelings in Washington. He really took me to the woodshed. When he finished I pointed out that I had merely told the concessionaires they couldn't assume that Senator Wallop's views were the unanimous views of Congress and that they needed to keep alert to changes to the concessions law that might be proposed by other members of Congress. I stood behind what I had said. I meant no disrespect to Senator Wallop but I wanted the concessionaires to go home with a more realistic picture of the situation. I still think I did the right thing and I hope Senator Wallop agrees.

Changing the concessions regulations proved to be emotional, complex, misunderstood and highly press-worthy. Congress was interested in what we were doing. I got strong signals from Senator Dale Bumpers of Arkansas, who served on the Energy and Natural Resources Committee, and Congressman Mike Synar of Oklahoma, who served on the Government Operations Committee, that they wanted to see reform, and if it didn't go far enough, they would push legislation to change the system.

There were two key provisions of the concessions regulations that were particularly difficult to understand. These provisions were the major impediments to encouraging any competition for concessions rights in the bidding process. One dealt with the definition of possessory interest, the other with preferential rights for incumbent concessionaires. As they were being administered, these provisions for all intents and purposes gave the incumbent a government-subsidized monopoly.

Granting a possessory interest to a concessionaire started out as a good idea. No private entity can build a building on government land and hold title to it. The government owns it the minute it's built. This put the concession company in a bad position. It couldn't go to the bank and borrow money to build something it wouldn't own. As a way around this, the concessionaire was granted a possessory interest so that bankers would lend money for construction projects. In the early days this was absolutely essential to attract private capital to the parks.

The idea is still good today. People are not going to risk private capital without some guarantees that they will be compensated for their investments if they lose their contracts. Fair enough. What wasn't fair was that concessionaires were getting contracts that defined possessory interest at fair market value or sound value. Both definitions were far too generous to the concessionaire and served as an effective roadblock to anyone who might want to compete for the business once the present contract was over.

Fair market value was defined, as you might surmise, by whatever the market would bear. Sound value was defined as being the cost of reconstruction of the facility less the amount of any visible depreciation. Anyone else bidding for the concession would have to compensate the incumbent for this value. At parks such as Yellowstone and Yosemite with all their concession buildings, this would be prohibitively expensive. No wonder we didn't get competition in the bidding process.

If the Park Service decided that a concessionaire was not performing up to standard and ruled it unsatisfactory, it could terminate the company's contract but would have to come up with the money to buy out its possessory interest. You can see why the Park Service was reluctant to find a concessionaire unsatisfactory. Where was it going to get the money to buy the concessionaire out? It was a bad situation.

Secretary Lujan made the point that a forced buyout actually cost the taxpayer three times: once when the concession company was given a very good deal to encourage it to do business in the parks; twice as the company wrote off all the depreciation of its buildings against its tax liability; and the third time when the government had to buy it out at an inflated-market or near-market value.

The definition of possessory interest was usually enough to discourage bids against a concessionaire. But just in case another bid came in, the incumbent was given the preferential right to match it. The incumbent could bid ridiculously low in the expectation that there would be no other bidder, and at worst could be required to raise its payment to the government to a more reasonable amount.

The concessionaires had a very advantageous situation and fought very hard to keep it. Yes, the Park Service was being taken to the cleaners, but most of the deals had been signed twenty or thirty years ago and the chance to change them was just coming up.

We made a number of changes, but the key ones had to do with the provisions I've just described. The Park Service would still grant possessory interest, but they would be calculated at book value, just as you would account for the interest in a new building in the private sector. The concessionaire would place the value of a new building on the books and start a depreciation schedule. Any buyout would be at the depreciated value rather than at the bloated "appreciated" value. The same value would be used in calculating a fair purchase price if another company were to win the contract and buy the incumbent concessionaire out.

We had to get creative in defining preferential rights. There are those who think that only Congress can change the definition, but we changed it. Maybe the courts will tell the Park Service it lacks this authority. If that happens, I guarantee that Congress will consider legislation to change the definition or take preferential rights away entirely.

The change we made hinged on two key words: *responsive bid*. What we said was that all bidders must be responsive to the conditions the Park Service sets out in the bid document. Under the previous definition, an incumbent could ignore many of the conditions and get away with it—after all, there wasn't going to be any competition. Now, if the incumbent is not willing to make a bid that is responsive to all the conditions of the bid document and a competitor submits a responsive bid, the incumbent loses its right of preference unless it submits a new bid that is responsive to all the conditions and is at least as good as the competitive bid.

This is a subtle change but is critical to any understanding of the new system. It puts the shoe on the Park Service's foot. The NPS can tell bidders what they must do to be responsive. It might be something like demanding that so much money be put into the upkeep in the park. It might be an investment in a new parking lot. It might be any number of items that would be in the best interest of the park. If the incumbent is not interested in meeting *all* the conditions and someone else is, the park will have a new, responsive concessionaire.

Concessions reform was not easy. It took us almost all of my four-year tenure to put this new system in place. There are members of Congress who want to "bulletproof" the new regulations by enacting them into law to make sure that a new administration doesn't weaken the intent of the changes. However, I would suggest that Congress let the system operate under the new regulations for a few years to see how they work out.

One final point: These new regulations will need to have common-sense interpretation. They are not "one size fits all." It was obvious to me from the start that the regulatory climate for the massive Park and Curry Company at Yosemite shouldn't be the same as for the small boat- and canoe-rental operators on the Chesapeake and Ohio Canal. There is a need for good faith, understanding and discussion to reach reasonable conclusions for such vastly different operations.

Although concessions reform was one of the most time-consuming things I did, I'm convinced the time was well spent. I feel we put the Park Service in charge of park concessions, which had not been the case before.

14

Yosemite Park & Curry Company

The story of the takeover of the Music Corporation of America (MCA) and its subsidiary, the Yosemite Park and Curry Company, could be a high-powered novel full of international intrigue. How we dealt with the principal Yosemite concessionaire changed the way the National Park Service will do business with all concessionaires in the future. It was among the most important accomplishments of my four years as director.

Was it a good deal for the American taxpayer? The government got $700,000 to $1 million a year from the old concessionaire. We will get an estimated $20 million a year from the new concessionaire—all to benefit the park. If this isn't a good deal, I don't know what is.

A quick summary to set the stage: The Yosemite Park and Curry Company was owned by the giant MCA of movie and recording fame. MCA was being bought out by Matsushita of Japan. These negotiations started secretly during the summer of 1990. The Park and Curry Company, whose gross sales were running in the $80 million range annually, was small potatoes in the overall deal.

Former senator Howard Baker and his firm of Baker, Worthington, Crossley, Stansberry and Woolf were serving as counsel to MCA as was the firm of Aiken, Gump, Strauss, Hauer and Feld. Bob Strauss, former national chairman of the Democratic Party, was leading the effort for Aiken Gump. It was widely reported that Strauss was earning his firm an $8 million fee for his work. Baker was getting somewhat less. I figured Strauss was hired to keep the Democrats quiet and Baker to do the same for the Republicans. There were more Democrats, so it was only fair that Strauss got more!

Ed Williams is a member of the Baker firm and a prince of a guy with a great deal of enthusiasm for the parks. I know him well and respect him. Baker's firm naturally chose Ed to contact me, who as Park Service director had to approve all transfers of concession ownership. That initial contact stretched out to more than two years of intense negotiations.

Park and Curry was in the twenty-seventh year of a thirty-year contract. When the contract was written, little of the infrastructure that now exists had been built at Yosemite and few government administrators foresaw how big this business would get. Under the contract Park and Curry was paying the government three quarters of 1 percent of gross sales for the privilege of operating in the park. Maybe that was reasonable when it was negotiated, but having to pay only 75 cents out of every $100 you take in would make anyone's mouth drool today. A clause in the contract said Park and Curry could renegotiate every five years, but who would want to renegotiate with a deal like that?

We wanted to renegotiate. I knew renegotiation would be in the best interest of the taxpayer and I honestly thought that Curry would be better off paying a more reasonable amount. Its ridiculously low percentage looked bad and was bad, and the press was beginning to understand and write about it. But we got nowhere with Curry's president, Ed Hardy. He is one of those "I was here when you came and will be here after you leave" guys and didn't want me messing in his affairs.

As it turned out, he might have helped not only himself but all the rest of the concessionaires if he hadn't taken such a hard line. His recalcitrance focused attention on the whole business of park concessions. With the strong urging and backing of Secretary Lujan, a new way of doing business with the parks was born.

But back to the MCA buyout. At first we picked up a few signals that MCA might give us Park and Curry as a goodwill gesture for all its years of operation in Yosemite. But some sharp accountant probably figured out that the gift would be too big to write off against MCA's losses. I had heard rumors of foreign investors buying American companies and loading them with all the debt for their acquisition to minimize their profit for U.S. tax purposes. I'm not suggesting this was

Matsushita's plan, but I wondered why the idea of a gift to the U.S. government for a tax write-off didn't make sense to them.

With the gift possibility growing dim, we began thinking about how to value Park and Curry for a sale. This wasn't easy, as the company had only three years of its contract left and had no idea what the conditions of a new contract might be. If it were able to renew its present sweetheart deal, the company was speculated to be worth well over $300 million. But it wasn't going to get that deal again while Secretary Lujan and I were there. And MCA needed to move promptly.

Ed Hardy was quoted as saying that the company's value was well above $200 million. I knew it would take more than that to replace its buildings; replacing just the Ahwahnee Hotel would cost nearly that much, and there were more than five hundred lesser structures. But I told Ed his company was only worth whatever the terms of the new contract would be. An old Marine—it was written all over him—Ed turned a few shades redder than the Marine Corps dress uniform.

I began to think about the idea of the government buying Park and Curry. If we could get the company for the right price we could pick a new operator, pay it a reasonable amount to operate the concessions, and put the profits back in the park. Not a bad idea, but the Park Service didn't have the money and I didn't have the authority. Minor problems!

My next thought was to have a nonprofit acquire the company. The National Park Foundation, chartered by Congress to help the parks, could buy the company's stock on the day its contract ended and immediately sell it to a qualified buyer. A problem here was that you got not only the assets but the liabilities, which were hard to calculate. There were underground storage tanks that had to be replaced and a minor difficulty related to some dumping the company had done years ago in a landfill.

I called Alan Rubin, president of the National Park Foundation, and told him he would make an ideal buyer. I think Alan fell out of his chair, although when he caught his breath he agreed it was an interesting concept. Yet the foundation had never taken on a deal such as this, and we still had no price.

Meanwhile the negotiations between MCA and Matsushita were heating up and getting lots of press. Secretary Lujan and I were both quoted that we would rather see the Park and Curry Company remain in American hands. Some accused us of Japan bashing, but I told a congressional committee I would take the same position if a British company were trying to take over Independence Hall.

There were more lawyers running around than could be reasonably tolerated. I met with Secretary Lujan and discussed what was going on. I was plowing new ground and needed any advice I could get. He suggested we go to California and meet directly with Lew Wasserman, MCA's chairman. Maybe we could work something out. The secretary was still thinking about that onetime proposal of a gift.

I was dumb enough to think I could call Wasserman and get an appointment. I was lucky he even took the call. He was very polite but seemed astonished that we would want to talk to him. After all, he was paying huge sums to have Strauss and Baker handle the transaction. This kind of business just wasn't done by principals meeting face to face.

Less than an hour after I talked with Lew Wasserman, Secretary Lujan got a call from Howard Baker saying that he and Bob Strauss wanted to come right over. Baker sounded unhappy. He and Strauss arrived with their game faces on and launched into a verbal assault that nearly blistered the varnish on the secretary's desk. They were angry with me for calling Wasserman directly and not going through them. They were angry that the secretary was publicly saying some things that might screw up the entire MCA deal, reported to be worth $7 billion. Although the Park and Curry part of the deal was small potatoes, the Matsushita people were very concerned about adverse press, and the secretary and I were flies in the ointment.

Howard Baker was plainly upset but maintained a gentleman's composure. I thought I could detect a twinkle in Bob Strauss's eye, but his language was much stronger. (He must have picked it up from hanging around with LBJ too much.) At one point Strauss let us know that they, and they alone, would decide what was to happen to the Park and Curry Company. I vividly remember one remark: "Hell, we will give the company to f—ing Saddam Hussein if we want to!"

This was before the Persian Gulf War, but even then Saddam wasn't on our "most admired" list. I couldn't believe Bob Strauss said it! Afterward I told the secretary we ought to leak word that Strauss had considered giving Yosemite's concessionaire to Saddam Hussein but that the secretary and I had turned him down. Wouldn't that have made a good *Washington Post* story?

Now the negotiations had become deadly serious. *Deadly* is the wrong word, but the intensity level went up and up. Lars Hanslin, a fine lawyer in our Solicitor's Office, was doing his best for us on this case, but he and I needed more help against the corporate giant.

Congress was beginning to get very interested in the situation. Senator Dale Bumpers of Arkansas, chairman of the Senate subcommittee on parks, asked me to come to his office to brief him on what was going on. Senator Bumpers is a powerful supporter of the parks and I wanted to make sure he was comfortable with our course of action.

I know he was concerned I might be getting in over my head with all those big businessmen and high-priced lawyers. I told him I was getting good advice from some National Park Foundation board members. The senator asked who they were, and I mentioned Neil Harlan, the board's vice chairman and the retired head of McKesson Corporation. He sat up in his chair. "The Snake knows about this deal?" he asked. I didn't know who the Snake was, I said, but Neil Harlan was with me every step. "The Snake was my college roommate," the senator explained. "If he's in on this I feel a lot more comfortable." So did I.

I returned to the foundation for more help. They loaned me Leonard Silverstein, a great guy who happened to know Lew Wasserman. We filled in the board members on the twists and turns of the pending transaction. Jim Harvey, chairman of TransAmerica, was another rock to cling to as I ventured into the depths of corporate intrigue. He found people who were willing to get involved pro bono because they loved Yosemite and enjoyed a good fight. Investment banker Tully Friedman was among them. Tully lobbed hand grenades into the MCA camp while we were busy trying to figure out a reasonable price to pay for the Park and Curry Company. Whatever intensity there was before, Tully doubled it.

Finally the MCA people sent in a team to see if we could reach agreement. They came to my office and started talking about $120 million. I asked them how they came up with that figure and they really had no answer. If they could make up a figure so could I. Besides, I was getting tired of all this mystery and intrigue. I'm afraid my language went the Bob Strauss route as I told them they were wasting my time and theirs, and that if they couldn't come back the next day with a number starting with four, not to come back.

The next day they came back with a number that was around $60 million. I said we were getting closer but I still wanted to buy for under $50 million and besides, I had no money. That made the conversation more interesting. How about Matsushita loaning the National Park Foundation the money until the existing contract is up and a new buyer is in place? This suggestion appeared to have merit. A few closed-door phone calls were made and the concept was approved.

The MCA people offered to sell the company for about $56 million and loan the foundation the money at 8 percent. The rate came from consulting that morning's *Wall Street Journal* and would be indexed to treasury bill rates. I asked how much higher the rate would need to be to bring the sale price below $50 million. A numbers cruncher concluded that 8.5 percent could justify a price of $49.5 million. We had a deal! Of course, there were lots of details for the lawyers to clean up. I figured they were getting paid enough to want to stretch this thing out as long as possible. Believe me, they kept the meter running.

We had just made the biggest financial deal in Park Service history. We were gaining a lot of tangible assets, but even more important, we were gaining control over the concessionaire who played a dominant role in one of our flagship parks.

As we were sitting at the table with the MCA people, Leonard Silverstein and I had a whispered conversation. We agreed that now might be a good time to ask MCA for a donation to the National Park Foundation, which uses such gifts for the good of the parks and the Park Service. I suggested to the group that we take a break before coming back to wrap up the meeting.

Leonard and I put our heads together in the hall. "How much should we ask for?" Leonard wondered. "I don't know," I replied. "How about a million dollars a year for each of the years remaining in their contract?" Leonard asked. "Let's try two million per year," I said. "After all, at one point they were talking about giving us the whole company."

Back in the conference room, I thanked everyone for working so hard to bring this deal to a close. There were smiles all around the table. I thought the American taxpayers would be well served by the deal, I said, and by the way, how would MCA feel about making a small contribution to the National Park Foundation as a token of appreciation for the many fine years of service the Park and Curry Company had given Yosemite's visitors? All chitchat stopped as the leader of the MCA negotiating team looked at me with a suspicious eye. "What size token do you have in mind?" he asked. "Two million dollars a year over the next three years would really help the parks," I answered with my heart in my throat. "Sounds okay to us," came the reply. I was in seventh heaven.

I figured we were going to make the government $15 to $20 million per year on the next contract. Surely I deserved a commission for my part in this achievement, but someone reminded me that Uncle Sam didn't pay commissions. I would have been happy just picking up the change falling out of Bob Strauss' pockets! However, the thrill of knowing that we landed a deal that would benefit both the American taxpayer and our beloved Yosemite was payment enough.

139

Part Five

The Threatened Ecology of Our Parks

15

The Everglades

I once asked a 40-year NPS veteran to name the most interesting parks he had served in. This fellow had served in almost every part of the country in a wide variety of parks. There was no hesitation in his answer. "If you are asking about scenic beauty you can't beat Glacier National Park. If your interest is in science, you can't beat the Everglades."

In terms of the popular press, the Everglades gathers its share of headlines right along with Yellowstone, Yosemite and the Grand Canyon. I think it is the most endangered of the national parks and is the best example of a park that cries for an ecosystem approach to management.

Located on the southern tip of Florida, it is the natural kidney for all the waters that flow to the south and into Florida Bay. The Everglades have been the cleansing sponge of South Florida for more years than we can count. For a system that has been as abused as the Everglades, it is a wonder there is life remaining in this "river of grass."

Marjory Stoneman Douglas, in her book *The Everglades: River Of Grass*, drew the nation's attention to the plight of South Florida. Mrs. Douglas, now over one hundred years old, has been a critic of the unnatural approach to managing the natural ecosystem since the 1940s. I have met with Mrs. Douglas and have found her to be a remarkable person. She is nearly blind and has some difficulty getting around, but put a microphone in her hand and she can still rally a crowd with her love of the Glades. When President Bush scheduled a trip to the Everglades we made sure that Marjory Stoneman Douglas had a place of honor from which to greet the president.

The pressure for growth in all of Florida and South Florida in particular has been intense. With the invention of air conditioning, this semitropical paradise has suffered from a rate of rapid growth that has taxed the ability of government planners beyond their limits. The result has been poorly planned growth and development—and the victim has been the natural environment of Florida.

Think of the Everglades as nature's thermometer for the state of Florida. In this case, the thermometer is capable of measuring the health of many things, but most important are the air and water. If the health of the Everglades is threatened then the health of the more populated areas outside the park's boundaries is threatened as well.

An entire book could be written on the insults to the natural systems of Florida by developers aided by an enthusiastic congressional delegation and an eager U.S. Army Corps of Engineers. The state capital, Tallahassee, is in the northernmost part of the state and was so far removed from where most of the damage during the early "boom" days of development was taking place that either the lawmakers didn't know or didn't care what was happening to the big old swamp in the south.

To the credit of the few around who understood the importance of the Glades, the public has finally begun to understand that as goes the health of the Everglades, so goes the health of South Florida. The NPS has long identified this park as a key scientific park and some of the best scientific minds in the NPS system have been assigned to the Everglades. I recognized the need to keep a strong management team in the park and was pleased that we had one of our most able superintendents, Mike Finley, assigned there.

Mike is a go-getter and was in a park that commanded daily press coverage. He kept the pot stirred, and on many occasions he was close to stepping over the line as to what a superintendent can or should say without consulting his boss, which in this case was Bob Baker, the regional director for NPS in Atlanta.

I decided I had better put the Everglades on my early visit list to get a personal view of what was going on in the park and to assess the leadership role Mike was playing in the community. After an initial briefing, Mike got me up in the air to get a view of the situation. From the air it was fairly obvious what all the artificial dikes, levees, and impoundments were doing to the whole South Florida area. Parts of the ecosystem were being starved of the water they needed to maintain some semblance of a natural balance, and other parts were being flooded and drowned with contaminated water from the north.

That contaminated water wasn't solely the product of overdevelopment. Intensive agriculture is a major contributor, with runoff from large cattle operations and the fields of the sugar producers causing the most damage. Superintendent Finley wanted my support in continuing to raise these issues in public forums at every opportunity. I was under some pressure in Washington to "corral" Finley as there were those in Secretary Lujan's office who thought Mike shot from the hip a little more than he should.

The truth is that I thought so too but I could see that he was up against a powerful coalition of developers and agribusiness interests that had had their way in Florida for a long time, and if Mike didn't occasionally shoot from the hip, the NPS might not get off any shots at all.

Mike needed to keep his regional boss and me informed of the issues and the positions that he intended to take. It is uncomfortable to catch hell in Washington over every press clip in the Miami paper without at least having a general understanding of the issues. I was willing to twist the tail of the developers and agribusiness interests, but I wanted the best information based on the best possible science we could produce to back our hand.

All through the four years I was director I was pleased to get the help and support of Florida Governors Bob Martinez and Lawton Chiles, along with key staff of President Bush. Both governors took a lot of heat from the strong lobbies of the developers and the agribusiness interests but held firm on the view that the Everglades needed the strong support of the state. If you search through press clips of the Bush years, you will find that the president spent many relaxing hours fishing near and in the Everglades, and we worked to make sure the president understood what was happening to one of his favorite fishing holes.

With Mike continuing to push the issue, and the U.S. Justice Department deciding the time was right and the evidence NPS had gathered was good enough to make a case in court, the tide of public opinion shifted in our direction in leaps and bounds. We were on a roll when Mike called me to indicate he would be interested in an opening we

145

were going to have for the superintendency of Yosemite—another park that shows up in the press on a regular basis.

Mike felt he had done about all he could do at the Everglades and he had personal reasons for wanting to head west. I thought Mike would make an excellent choice for Yosemite, but I could sense an environmental-interest-group backlash if they thought Mike was being taken out of the Everglades because of the pressure of the developers and the agribusiness interests. I told Mike that he could go if he won the support of the western regional director, Stan Albright, but not until he had made contact with the key environmental leaders to let them know he was leaving because he wanted to go—not because he was being forced out.

We were fortunate to have Bob Chandler, another very capable NPS veteran, willing to take the leadership of the Everglades as Mike took off. Bob is a little less flamboyant than Mike but every bit as effective. I wanted a strong leader with good public relations skills in that job as the pressure continued to mount. Bob was the right guy. We didn't miss a beat as we continued to press for an environmental cleanup of the South Florida mess.

Unfortunately, Bob's wife had a difficult time with the climate of South Florida. Apparently her health would be better served in a drier climate. It wasn't long until Bob knew that he would have to leave, but he hung in there through some of the toughest times until he requested a transfer. He had done all that I had asked of him under difficult conditions and while I hated to see him leave, the health of his family was too important to jeopardize.

I am confident that the combination of a very strong public education program that has long been a point of pride for the Everglades staff and the growing awareness of the public across this country, coupled with the waking up of the bureaucracy at both the state and federal level, will keep this issue of the environmental health of Florida on the front burner. The new superintendent, Dick Ring, arrived just in time to get settled when Hurricane Andrew struck, doing great damage to much of the park and completely destroying the new home where he had just moved.

The devastation to the park and that entire area of Florida was something that I have never seen or ever want to see again. The majority of our employees lost their homes and all their possessions. The natural environment of the park rode out the storm pretty well; it was the man-made environment that took the most damage. This was a tough situation for a new superintendent to step into. For the record, Dick Ring did a great job of holding his park together under the most trying times. His ability to carry on under the toughest of circumstances gives me confidence that he will carry on in the tradition of the long line of outstanding superintendents who have led Everglades.

The clean water and clean air fight is not over in South Florida, but it is headed in the right direction and the momentum is building. As I write this chapter the fight has intensified in the Florida legislature. There is no argument that the agricultural interests are going to have to pay for a major part of the cleanup of the Glades. The question comes down to how much. There is talk that the plan to clean up the Glades will cost somewhere in the neighborhood of $685 million over the next twenty years, and that the growers would pay approximately $233 million to $322 million of this cost. This money would be used to create a forty-thousand-acre "kidney" or series of marshes that would strain the impurities coming off the agricultural lands.

This fight is not over yet. When you throw around numbers that are that big for a cleanup, you can assume the taxpayer will have to cough up a significant portion of the total. The dynamics of who will pay, and how much, are still very much up in the air.

Even the powerful lobby of the developers and the sugar interests will not be able to resist the move to clean up the state. The issue has become more than just a state or national issue. Even the eyes of the international community are focused on the health of the Everglades, and it is up to us to demonstrate that we have the will and the ability to undo the wrongs we have done in Florida.

16

The Yellowstone Fires, Geysers & Ecosystem

Although the Yellowstone fires of 1988 had been out more than six months when I took office, the embers were still hot. As I made my way around the Hill with congressional visits, one of the topics that members wanted to discuss most was fire philosophy.

Bob Barbee, Yellowstone's superintendent, became a media event during those times as every reporter wanted a word from the park's top man. Bob is the picture of a rugged western park superintendent and handled the press as well as he could, which was pretty well.

The Yellowstone fires burned approximately 800,000 acres in the park. The area burned grew to more than a million acres when you added in the fires burning throughout the ecosystem. Hot, dry conditions fanned by sixty-mile-per-hour winds whipped these fires into a frenzy. Despite man's best efforts, to say that these fires were under control is stretching it a bit. Until the snows of September 1988 fell, the fires went about anywhere they wanted to.

Of course, they became a huge media event and resurrected old arguments about fighting every fire from day one versus allowing some fires to burn. One of the Yellowstone researchers had set out a test plot to evaluate the impact of fire on all the various things growing there and the regenerative powers of the land. For the research to be successful the test plot needed to burn. The fire was nearing his test plot and the researcher, hoping the fire would reach it, pleaded aloud, "Burn, baby, burn." Unfortunately, there were also media people nearby. Guess what quote the media decided to use? There on network news was our employee seemingly urging all of Yellowstone to "Burn, baby, burn." Needless to say, a number of members of Congress reminded me of that news bit and speculated that the entire Park Service had a "Burn, baby, burn" attitude.

There are two things that need clearing up. First, the Park Service, in cooperation with other government agencies, fought those fires aggressively. True, they may have started the fight a little slowly, but as soon as the fires escalated the fire-fighting effort grew intense.

Given the intensity of the fires coupled with hot, dry weather and gusting winds, there was little the world's best firefighters could do to control this inferno. The fire was jumping normal firebreaks and leap-frogging ahead as much as half a mile. You couldn't build a firebreak big enough to stop it no matter how many bulldozers you had.

Kyle Ridenour with a backdrop of burned-over wilderness in Yellowstone. I snapped this picture from the front of the canoe. My son Kyle and I had canoed into the wilderness on Lake Yellowstone. We were there to get a look at what the fires had done to the park—and to catch a few of those famous cutthroat trout.

The second and more important point is that the fires wouldn't have been so intense if there hadn't been so much forest litter on the forest floor. You won't get the really big fire if little fires have burned through and consumed the downed limbs and fallen trees. Periodic fires keep these fuel sources down.

So after all the bitter argument, the answer still is that fires are a necessary part of our ecosystem and always have been. Yellowstone burned many times before man ever set eyes on it. There has to be coordination among agencies and strict guidelines as to when and where fires will be allowed to burn, but fighting all fires aggressively from day one would be a very expensive proposition as well as a mistake in terms of the health of the forest.

A closing note on Yellowstone fires: In the summer of 1991, I stopped in for a short visit to Yellowstone. A fire of about fifteen thousand acres was burning in a northeasterly direction along the Pelican Valley. Chief Ranger Dan Sholly was there to greet me and to explain the situation. Of course, the television crews were scurrying about, hoping for a big story.

Dan asked me, "Boss, how do you want to fight this thing?" I suggested that we get up in a helicopter and get a good look at it. From the air the answer was obvious. The fire was burning toward an old, burned-out area where there would be little fuel for it.

I asked Dan for his suggestions. After explaining what he thought would happen to the fire given the moisture conditions and its destination, Dan said: "We can fight it like hell for about two million dollars, or we can drag around a lot of hose and kick up a lot of dust and appear to be fighting it like hell for about two hundred thousand. The result will be the same either way, but with all the press...?"

I chose the $200,000 solution. As far as I know, the press never knew and the American taxpayers saved a bunch of money.

Another "hot" issue concerns the great natural geysers and bubbling hot springs of Yellowstone, which have attracted visitors—man and animal—to the area long before recorded time. Tales of these mystical, almost magical features reached unbelieving ears in the East from early fur traders and adventurers. It was not until the photography of William Jackson and the paintings of George Catlin reached the Washington scene that the idea of protecting this area as a park led to President Grant's setting aside the area in 1872.

This great attraction to Old Faithful and the many other geologic features has brought millions of visitors to the park over the years. It was no wonder that the NPS got nervous when the Church Universal and

Triumphant wanted to drill into the geothermal features outside the park's boundaries near Gardiner. The church's leaders could see many uses for the geothermally heated steam and hot water as a source of energy for their followers. I didn't blame them.

On the other hand, what if they drilled into the features and accidently hit a vein that allowed the pressure to escape from beneath the park's features? I couldn't tolerate being the man who stood by and watched Old Faithful dry up—or even become less faithful.

Of course, we commissioned a study by the United States Geological Survey (USGS)—the world's experts on these matters. The USGS study was exhaustive. The team tried every technique known to man in an effort to see if there was any possible connection between the proposed drilling site and the park's features.

In a high-level meeting at Interior I got the results of the study. To make a much longer story short, the USGS scientists thought it highly unlikely that any harm would come from allowing the church to drill within certain parameters. The parameters: that the church would not withdraw more water than what would flow naturally from the spring near the proposed well site.

I questioned the scientists at great length. How sure were they? Were they absolutely, positively sure? I wanted the strongest assurances possible. They gave me what were in their minds the strongest possible assurances— but they could not be *absolutely* sure.

I pointed out to them that the NPS had received information counter to their conclusions from a member of their own agency, housed in Denver. He had much stronger feelings about the possibility that the drilling could cause problems. They dismissed the Denver colleague's concern with an attempt to discredit his scientific capability. Scientists disputing scientists—that was just what I needed.

My decision was easy. I had always said that if there was any doubt I would err on the side of protecting the resource. This was not a new policy for me. It was the backbone of my philosophy on protecting the features of the parks. I opted not to allow the drilling.

My decision was issued in the form of a recommendation to the secretary of Interior. I was not surprised to be overturned as the case the

USGS scientists made was very strong. I couldn't blame Secretary Lujan for his decision. He had urged that we go with the best scientific information possible—but the USGS was unwilling to give the assurances I needed to go with its recommendation.

As you can imagine, the issue got hot politically and politicians were scrambling for polling information that would tell them which side of the issue was best to come down on if they wanted to get reelected. Since the Church Universal and Triumphant was having its share of conflicts with other residents of Montana, it soon became clear that the best position for the Congress was to—you guessed it—ban the drilling until further studies could be made.

Yellowstone has another controversial issue brewing. That is the possibility of a gold mine being located at Cooke City, just outside the north boundary. There are all kinds of questions that must be answered. These are not just park questions; they are ecosystem questions. What will happen to the streams? Is there going to be a significant sedimentation problem? Are there air quality problems associated with the mining operation and all the vehicles associated with the mine? What does the project mean in terms of infrastructure demand such as roads, sewers and schools?

The point is that projects like this can no longer be considered in isolation. The ripple of a rock thrown into a pond moves in all directions. The location of an energy-intensive mining operation in the Yellowstone ecosystem sends ripples in every direction.

There has been talk about managing the Yellowstone area with an ecosystem approach to management for years. With all or parts of seven national forests surrounding the park, it only makes sense. The wildlife and the vegetation of the area have no knowledge of artificial political boundaries between the state and federal governments nor of the lines between national forests and the park.

In recent years we have been relatively fortunate to have superintendents and forest supervisors who, more or less, understand this concept of ecosystem awareness and work at creating a cooperative attitude in decision making impacting the area. This has not always been the case, nor has it ever been the official policy of the federal government, but

153

good, common-sense management is ecosystem management and both the Forest Service and the NPS have had good leadership in the Yellowstone area.

The term *ecosystem management* scares many of the more conservative Westerners to death. They jump to the conclusion that ecosystem management is a park system term that means that the U.S. forests in the area of Yellowstone are going to be taken over by the park and run under park system rules, and that the multiple-use characteristics of forest management will go by the wayside. Even some Forest Service employees think that. It might be that some NPS employees think that as well.

From left to right—Interior Secretary Manuel Lujan; Judy Bracken; Jim Ridenour; Deputy Sectetary Frank Bracken; John Varley, chief scientist, Yellowstone. John is giving us a lecture on why buffalo roam and wolves howl.

I never thought it and don't think it now. There is absolutely no reason why the Forest Service and the NPS should adopt identical management policies for the units under their supervision in Yellowstone. They should, however, be working toward cooperative management policies that bring out the best in each unit while strengthening the eco-system as a whole. In many speeches and articles I have urged the "blur-ring of the lines" between the federal land management agencies. Yellowstone is one of those places where blurring of the lines makes the most sense—and the sooner the better.

The concept needn't frighten the multiple-use advocates. Multiple use as a philosophy doesn't have to disappear. A radical, overnight policy shift doesn't have to occur. What needs to occur is that our governmen-tal leaders need to look at decisions within the ecosystem in a common-sense, cooperative manner. Communicate and plan together along with the public when making decisions about new campground sites. Work with local tourism and environmental groups when planning trail sys-tems. Work with farmers and ranchers to reach win-win positions.

Yes, the grazing and mining laws that stretch back to 1872 are going to have to be modified. But the changes needn't be so radical as to totally disrupt generations of lifestyles. The ecosystem is not in such bad shape that everything has to change tomorrow, but common-sense change should not be put off. Each journey begins with a step.

I may be making this sound too easy but it isn't as difficult as we have been led to believe. We have a big head start because the various state and federal units in the area have been working in this direction for a number of years.

17

Wolves in Yellowstone

Reintroducing wolves to Yellowstone was a hot topic when I came to Washington and it was just as hot when I left. People were either for it or against it and they weren't shy about voicing their opinion.

Specifically we are talking about *Canis lupus*, the species that had survived in the greater Yellowstone ecosystem for hundreds if not thousands of years. There is a strong population of these wolves in Alaska and Canada. There has been a resident population in Minnesota for many years and there is a growing population in Montana. Generally these wolves have migrated down from Canada and are a rare sight in the lower forty-eight states.

The wolves were a nuisance to the early settlers and bounties for killing them were quite common in Western states as late as the 1920s. Wolves were thought to be extinct in the Yellowstone area by 1930.

On one of my first house-hunting trips in Virginia I saw Senator Alan Simpson of Wyoming and his wife Ann taking a walk in the neighborhood I was investigating. I had met Senator Simpson but, following my rule, I stuck out my hand and reintroduced myself. Senator Simpson is one of my favorite senators as he has a good, common-sense approach to government and a quick wit. He asked me what I was doing in their neighborhood and I couldn't resist replying that I was looking for a place to reintroduce wolves. He got a big laugh out of that and said something like, "Better here than Wyoming." He also advised me not to lose my sense of humor—I would need it to survive in Washington.

The subject of wolf reintroduction came up again on one of my early congressional courtesy calls on Congressman Ron Marlenee of Montana. Ron was the ranking Republican on the parks subcommittee of the House Interior and Insular Affairs Committee, so he was an important person for me to get along with. Unfortunately our personalities clashed from the moment we met. I didn't care for his brow-beating, intimidating style and figured the less I saw of him the better off we both would be.

As I was ushered into his office I noticed a wolf hide stretched out in front of his desk. "Ridenour," he said, "the only way I want to see a wolf in Yellowstone is dead." Then he glowered at me during a long period of silence. I hadn't given the wolf issue much thought in my first few days as director and I wasn't about to make a major commitment to Congressman Marlenee with no more experience on the issue than a short briefing. We ended an awkward meeting and I went away thinking, This guy is not going to run over me, but how am I going to work with him?

A few months later he sent me a letter that was downright insulting. The first naval vessel the United States captured from Japan in World War II was a two-man submarine operating in Pearl Harbor on December 7, 1941. A group called the Pearl Harbor Survivors Association, made up of American military personnel who were at Pearl Harbor on that day, wanted the sub reconditioned and brought back to Hawaii to be part of the display somewhere in the area of the USS *Arizona* Memorial.

Other museums around the country wanted the sub but I felt that the most deserving and common-sense display area would be back in Hawaii where it was captured. Congressman Marlenee got interested in this subject, probably from constituents concerned that the sub not be placed in any way to look as if it had triumphed over *Arizona*. We understood the uneasiness and were working with everyone to find the right display situation. But Marlenee sent me a nasty letter questioning if I was a "red-blooded American." This irritated the hell out of me. I had served in Vietnam as a medic and my unit saved thousands of lives under difficult conditions. I was sure that the congressman had never served in battle. For him to question my loyalty was too much.

I responded in a note slightly less hostile in tone than his. He wanted a meeting with me; I refused. Finally he got Secretary Lujan to ask me if I would meet with him. I reluctantly agreed and went expecting an apology. Instead, Marlenee starting ripping me about the tone of my response. I was on the verge of challenging him to a duel, but instead I asked him to re-read the insulting letter he had sent me—which I guessed had been written by one of his off-the-wall staff. After he re-read the letter, he laid it down, glanced at a staffer across the room, and suggested we move on to different topics.

I don't know how this story got into my *Wolves in Yellowstone* discussion, but it does give me a chance to get Ron Marlenee off my chest. There are few people I can't get along with; he is one of them.

The possibility of reintroducing wolves to the Yellowstone area is complicated and tied up in layers of rules and regulations in the U.S. Fish and Wildlife Service. My good friend John Turner was head of that agency. He has an excellent education in wildlife biology and had become a politician of some note in his home state of Wyoming.

Under the law there are things that John had to do to protect wildlife species, but this idea of putting wolves in Yellowstone was a tough pill for him to swallow. His former political allies in Wyoming urged him to ignore his responsibilities and make sure that this reintroduction never occurred. John moaned to me that he would never be able to return to his home state if the reintroduction took place under his leadership of the Fish and Wildlife Service. I wished I could take some heat off him but the law was clear about which agency had to lead in reintroducing species. As Park Service director I would have some say about the use of the park as a host, but that was all.

The law talks about the use of an experimental population to see if reintroduction will work. In simple terms, you set aside an area where an experimental population of wolves is to be introduced. While the wolves stay within the boundaries of the area they are protected, but if they roam outside the boundaries they can be shot as predators. On the other hand, if wolves repopulate an area without the designation of an experimental population—if they come back on their own—they are protected under the Endangered Species Act and there are heavy fines and even possible prison sentences for those who shoot them.

Now comes the dilemma for Wyoming anti-wolf groups. What if wolves show up in the Yellowstone area without government help? Then those who risk shooting them are in big trouble. The anti-wolf people might be better advised to support an experimental reintroduction of

159

wolves within the borders of Yellowstone National Park. Then any wolf outside the park would be fair game.

Every few months someone would report sighting a wolf in the Yellowstone area. These reports were hard to verify—a hunter shot an animal he thought to be a coyote only to find out that it was a wolf or a cross-breed of some sort that had all the characteristics of a wolf. Were wolves repopulating the area naturally? Or were some of the pro-wolf groups trapping them in Canada and releasing them in Yellowstone?

That argument has not been settled. The controversy rages on. The reintroduction decision will be made in Congress and it won't be easy. The fight is about more than just wolves. It is a philosophical fight that reaches to individual and states' rights. Not until the issue has been thoroughly debated will a solution be found.

18

Oh, Give Me a Home Where the Buffalo Roam

Technically, we're not talking buffalo here—we're talking bison. I don't know that it makes much difference to anyone, but I was corrected for this technical error many times during my Park Service years and I want to make sure the biologists know I recognize the distinction.

The Park Service was having trouble with its neighbors, primarily in Montana. It seems that the bison didn't always want to stay on Yellowstone property and would get the urge to roam. Wasn't there a song written about this?

The problem was that some of the bison were infected with an old agricultural enemy—brucellosis. Brucellosis is a serious disease for a cattle rancher. It often causes the female cows to abort. If you are trying to build up a herd of fine cattle, that becomes a real problem.

It is an even bigger problem if you are in the business of breeding fine cattle. For example, if there is any sign that you have brucellosis in your herd, you will have a quarantine slapped on you and you can no longer ship cattle or semen from your fine bull in interstate commerce.

Montana had been certified as a brucellosis-free state and the agriculture people, both federal and state, were nervous about our infected bison mixing with the cattle grazing on mostly Forest Service land outside Yellowstone. The point that there had never been a proven case of transmission of brucellosis on the range from a bison to a cow had little impact on the concern of the cattlemen. A researcher down in Texas claimed to have penned up an infected bison with a cow and, after much encouragement, managed to get the cow infected. That was all the "proof" the ranchers wanted.

I can't say I blamed them. After all, most of those ranchers had their whole lives built upon the health of their herds and didn't want to take any chances.

We tried everything to keep the bison in Yellowstone. We tried herding them using rangers on horseback. We tried herding by helicopter. No matter what we tried, the bison seemed to get the urge to see new country.

I asked one of our scientists if the bison were leaving because they needed a better supply of food. After she provided a lot of big words and lengthy descriptions of bison genetics, I interrupted her: "What you are saying is the bison will roam when they get the urge." She had to agree. The old song had it right.

The range just north of the park was where the bison appeared to like to go. Perhaps that route was bred into them, or the grass looked greener there. This was the old Malcolm Forbes ranch. James Watt had the chance to buy that land pretty cheap during his time as Interior secretary. Instead, much of it was sold to Clare Prophet and the Church Universal and Triumphant.

Secretary Watt's negative decision cost the Park Service not one but three major headaches that are not solved to this day. One, the bison became trespassers as they left the park and headed north. Two, the church, known by the acronym CUT, moved in next door and became a major pain in the rear—not only for the Park Service but for all its neighbors. Three, CUT left Southern California where it had been a major pain in the rear and sold its property to a Japanese university—I say university with my tongue planted deeply in my cheek—which promptly became its own version of a pain in the rear to its neighbors and the Park Service. The controversy over CUT is still going on in the Santa Monica Mountains.

So without the land acquisition the bison roamed and the governor of Montana fretted. The Montana legislature decided to have a limited hunting season for bison. Under the law, the bison became the property of the state once they left the park.

The national news media soon took care of Montana's hunting season. The evening news would show pictures of some guy walking up to a bison near downtown Gardiner and dropping the beast from a few short yards away. No one ever said the bison was the most wily beast to hunt. Of course, this incensed the animal rights groups and all the East Coast viewers who thought the last bison in the world were biting the dust. As far as the Park Service was concerned, we were not worried about the numbers: The herd actually needed a little culling because bison no longer have any natural enemies. The ranchers had killed all the wolves—but that story is in the previous chapter.

The governor sent his staff to plead with us to do something. "What?" I asked. "Anything," he replied. The image of bloodthirsty Montana hunters on network news was bad for business. We went through committees and advisors like Sherman went through Georgia. Things would calm down for a while and then flare up, hot as ever.

After the governor dropped the hunting season, I suggested he allow the state game wardens to "harvest" the bison and give the meat to some worthy cause. He countered that the Park Service should harvest the bison because they were ours. I pointed out that they didn't belong to us—especially once they left the park. We compromised with a plan to send some of our best sharpshooters to help the state game wardens in the harvest and give the meat to local Native American tribes while the research to find a better solution would continue.

Not wanting the heat either, I asked Cy Jamison, director of the Bureau of Land Management, for a shipment of BLM uniforms for our shooters. He was rightly suspicious.

On a concluding note, I never could quite figure out why all our complaints from Montana were about bison. After all, the elk that ran in and out of the park had brucellosis also. Could it be that the powerful hunting lobby in Montana didn't want the word *elk* mentioned in this controversy? Those rich Easterners paid big bucks to bag elk!

19

Alaska

Since I probably spent more time on Alaska than any other state, it deserves a chapter by itself. The Park Service has a regional office just for Alaska and some people in Washington concentrate their entire effort on the state. Like the state, the opportunities and controversies there are big.

One reason for Alaska's unique status, I think, is that it didn't become a state until 1959, nearly half a century after the last of the lower forty-eight achieved statehood. The Alaska statehood law was tediously written to cover a wide variety of situations that weren't even thought of earlier. It was followed in 1971 by another complex law to settle the land claims of Alaska natives.

Another reason is Alaskans themselves, an interesting mix who make much of their differences from the rest of the country and each other. Among non-natives, some are libertarians who have moved there to get away from the smothering laws, rules and regulations that are part of daily life below the 49th parallel. Some have come because of their great love for Alaska's land and resources, making them extremely sensitive to environmental matters and intent on preserving our country's last great frontier. Some, dating back to the gold rush, have come to harvest and harness Alaska's great resources such as oil, coal and gas as well as the state's abundant wildlife. These factions are constantly on a collision course and small issues become major issues overnight.

Former Congressman Jim Jontz of Indiana discovered how strongly Alaskans feel about issues affecting them. I've known Jim for years, dating back to my time as director of Indiana's Department of Natural Resources while he was serving in the state legislature. An ardent environmentalist, he was elected from a very conservative district in Indiana because of his hard work as a campaigner and good service to his constituents. I knew he would not be able to maintain a high profile on environmental issues and serve his constituency very long—he was too far to the left of where the home folks were.

Sure enough, Jim couldn't resist becoming an advocate for major changes in the way timber was harvested in Alaska and other western states. Jim's opinions weren't generally appreciated by those states' representatives, who tended to feel that a freshman congressman from Indiana should worry about Indiana issues and let westerners take care of their own problems. They sent numerous shots across Jim's bow, but he was determined. Don Young, the lone congressman from Alaska, finally devised a way to send Jim an unmistakable signal. He introduced a bill to make Jim's entire district—covering much of northwestern Indiana—a national forest.

Don's bill focused attention on Jim, and it wasn't long until Westerners who depended on the timber industry decided to let the Hoosiers in Jim's district hear about what they thought of Jim's meddling in western affairs. Groups were actually organized in the Pacific Northwest to come to Indiana to campaign against him. The conservative farmers of his district shared many of the same feelings about federal government interference in state affairs, and that was the beginning of the end of Jim's elected career.

For the Park Service, it seemed that an issue of critical importance sprang up nearly every day from Alaska. One such issue was the question of how many cruise ships should be allowed into Glacier Bay.

Glacier Bay in Glacier Bay National Park is one of the most beautiful spots in the United States and a great place for whale watching. Naturally it's a favorite destination for cruise ships. We had limited the number of cruise ship entries into the bay primarily because we were concerned about possible disturbance of the humpback whale, but also about smokestack emissions and disturbance of other species.

We were allowing 107 entries over the ninety-day cruise ship season. That meant there would be two boats a day on some days but only one on others. Don't ask me how we arrived at that figure—there was no logical basis I could discover for it.

Senator Frank Murkowski of Alaska had a good argument for easing the restriction: From an environmental point of view, what better way to see a national park than from a boat? The land isn't disturbed. Trash stays on the boat and isn't scattered around the park. Nothing is taken but pictures. It was a very persuasive argument and one I couldn't ignore.

Many of our people opposed increasing cruise ship entries, fearing that more traffic in the bay would disturb the whales. But they had no solid evidence to substantiate this fear. Others believed that whales were influenced chiefly by food supply and said the area just outside the bay was better for whale watching despite having more traffic than the bay. Without adequate research data to reach a conclusion either way, we turned to the National Marine Fisheries Service (NMFS) for advice.

As I write this chapter the NMFS has said that under controlled conditions they see no reason why two cruise ships per day would be detrimental to the whales. The Park Service will get heavy pressure from all directions on this decision, but without clear evidence that it will cause a problem, the clamor for more cruise ships will be hard to resist.

The National Park Service now puts an education ranger on board each cruise ship to tell the story of the park. It gets one dollar per passenger for providing this service. My personal opinion is that the NPS should get at least five dollars per passenger from the cruise lines and that the money should go directly into the research program in the bay. The Park Service could temporarily raise the number of cruise ships allowed into the bay under this arrangement while setting up an extensive monitoring and inventorying system that will take the mystery out of the ship-impact issue.

As it is, the cruise ships are not leaving much money in Alaska. The cruise companies are foreign-owned. Food service, accommodations, entertainment and even souvenirs are all provided aboard ship. Ashore, the cruise passengers often travel in company-owned buses and stay in company-owned hotels. Little of what they spend gets to Alaskans. The cruise lines can afford to reinvest some of their revenues in the resource that is responsible for their business: Alaska!

Some Alaskans feel that too much of their state has been "locked up" in national parks accessible to and visited by too few people. Senator

Murkowski is fond of saying that there are more rangers than visitors in Alaska's parks. He tells the story of a couple who had gone to Alaska to celebrate their anniversary. They were really looking for a back-country experience, hoping to canoe and hike in solitude. When they got to the back country a park ranger greeted them. He was very courteous and probably felt he needed to keep an eye on the couple in case they got into trouble. Maybe he was lonely for some human company. In any event, the ranger tailed them at some distance throughout their entire trip. They weren't particularly angry, but their dream of a romantic trip of solitude was shaken.

Mining is another issue in the Alaska parks. Today's mining operations force thousands of gallons of water through powerful hoses to wash away overburden and get to the minerals. Streams fill up with mud, the land is scarred, and reclamation efforts are often ineffectual. Unless there is some sort of a national emergency, I would urge that the government buy out mining claims within the parks. It is only fair that claimants be compensated, but there should not be windfall profits.

In addition, miners should not be allowed to claim surface rights based on ownership of mineral rights. This practice has been a rip-off in this country for far too long. There are people who have acquired mineral rights and have no intention of ever developing them; their interest is in getting possession of the surface rights at ridiculously low prices. What they want to do on the surface scares me more than mining. I have visions of casinos stretching all across park lands in Alaska. This situation needs to be cleaned up before it gets out of hand.

*

People come from all over the world to climb Mount McKinley or, as Alaskans call it, Denali. In the 1992 climbing season eleven climbers lost their lives there. Changes in the weather were rapid and brutal and some climbers were ill-equipped and unprepared to handle such adversity. Nowhere is it more dangerous and costly to mount a rescue effort than in Alaska. With the extremes in climate, what starts out to be a nice hike can turn into a nightmare for the hiker and for those trying to find him or her.

To a ranger trained and dedicated in rescue work, the thought of trying to save a life is irresistible. But should we put the lives of rangers in peril to rescue someone who has made a foolish decision despite warnings and weather? What about risking lives to recover the remains of an unfortunate climber? The Park Service has often been asked to provide this service.

Park Service and military rescue efforts during 1992 cost in the millions. Should the taxpayer have to bear this cost? Perhaps those attempting to climb in dangerous areas should be required to have rescue insurance or to post bonds. Some argue that this wouldn't work and that the cost would make climbing a sport for the rich. My personal belief is that you accept certain risks when you get into these high-danger sports and should assume responsibility for the consequences. But there is no "one size fits all" answer to this problem, and I'm not prepared to offer a solution. This issue is a good one for all of us to consider.

I can't end a chapter on Alaska without a discussion of subsistence. Subsistence rights for native Alaskans have been confusing and controversial since they were guaranteed when Alaska became a state.

Everyone has a different idea of who is eligible for these rights and what the definition of subsistence should be. Some seem to think that the last person off the plane who states an intention to live in Alaska should have subsistence rights. If it wasn't so sad it would be funny to see these doctors, dentists and lawyers from Anchorage argue how they should be considered "native" and given full rights. I can buy that only if they have true native blood flowing through their veins.

And what does subsistence mean? My thought is that the lawmakers wanted to guarantee that those natives who lived off the land before statehood would not lose their traditional rights of hunting, fishing and gathering food for their families. Now we find people hunting and fishing commercially and wanting to call it subsistence. Their reasoning is that the need for subsistence has changed. They say they need cash to subsist and can only get it by intensifying their traditional native activities.

I can see the argument that native Alaskans want to provide educational opportunities for their children. They also want cars, televisions, snowmobiles and other modern conveniences. I just want to make sure that the intent to preserve a way of life is not subverted. Both the courts and the legislative bodies, state and federal, need to spend more time on this issue.

20

Air Quality in the Parks

People tend to think of national parks as pristine places where "we can get a breath of fresh air." Relatively speaking, they are correct, but the parks are part and parcel of the United States. There is no invisible border at the park boundary that keeps air pollution out.

I am hesitant to write this chapter. There are so many "experts" on air pollution around that you can find one inclined to testify to almost any opinion if you have the money to pay for it. That may sound a bit harsh, but I served as a member of the Air Pollution Control Board of Indiana for eight years, and I always wondered how air-quality scientists could so convincingly disagree on the impacts of pollution sources while studying the same basic facts of a permit application. In our public hearings, it seemed that each party to the discussion had the best expert available to tell us how we should vote. With so much disagreement among the scientific experts, it made voting tough for the lay board member.

The Park Service has a talented air-quality staff and is on the cutting edge of many clean air issues. One of the most complex issues relates to visibility. With all the great vistas in the parks, is it any surprise that NPS staff would be on the cutting edge on visibility issues? I can tell you from experience that it is often lonely on the cutting edge, and I am sure that the NPS air-quality staff would agree.

With my encouragement, the Park Service won a big fight over the gradual loss of visibility at Grand Canyon National Park. The Grand Canyon becomes less grand if you can't see it. Of course, this loss of visibility did not take place overnight and cannot be attributed to any one source of emissions. The loss is subtle and has taken place over the past eighty years. (At least the loss attributable to man has taken place in fairly recent times. Loss due to natural events such as volcanic eruptions can be traced over thousands of years.)

171

It has long been thought that much of the "haze" drifting into the Grand Canyon was coming from the land of the moving parking lot—Southern California. There is a great deal of truth to this, but it has been hard to pin down a specific culprit in such a large area. Certainly the increase in the number of cars, trucks and buses in the West has added significantly to the problems at the Grand Canyon. Many of our great western cities have felt this degrading impact of the combustion engine.

Our NPS researchers were especially interested in a haze that seemed to move into the canyon during the winter months. They joined with others to look for major emission sources. One of those sources turned out to be the Navajo Generating Station at Page, Arizona. This was a surprise, as Page is north and east of the canyon and one would think the prevailing winds would carry those emissions eastward, away from the canyon.

The Navajo Generating Station is a 2,250-megawatt, coal-fired power plant about twelve miles from the northern boundary of the park. The facility emits approximately seventy thousand tons of sulfur dioxide per year and is the second largest single source of sulfur dioxide in the western United States. By adding certain tracers into the stack emissions at Page, the NPS staff was able to track the emissions to the Grand Canyon. The evidence was there and hard to refute.

Adding advanced scrubber technology to the plant is estimated to cost more than $430 million and would add nearly $90 million in annual operating costs. The costs are high and the stakes are high.

There are six owners of the plant and one of them happens to be the Bureau of Reclamation, a sister agency of the NPS in the Interior Department. As you might imagine, BLM was not excited about the prospect of coming up with its share of $430 million to retrofit the plant with scrubbers. Things got a little tense in the halls of Interior as one scientific group argued with the other. Before long, this was not just an argument within the halls of Interior; it became a major issue for the Environmental Protection Agency and the White House. I was proud of the EPA and the White House staff as they supported the NPS position to add scrubber technology to the plant. To allow further degradation to the air quality at the Grand Canyon was unthinkable.

A similar issue came up when a major automobile manufacturer was looking for a new plant site near Great Smoky Mountains National Park. One of the prime considerations was concern about the additional emissions that would be put into the air of an area already heavily impacted from pollution-control problems. With economic times being tough, all the surrounding states were anxious to land this plant and the jobs it would bring their residents. Who could blame them?

Although the states make the decisions in these situations, the Park Service can have a big impact. People listen to its advice. The parks play a big role in tourism, and no state wants to jeopardize its appeal to tourists if it can possibly avoid it.

Probably the best thing that came out of the Park Service stance on this plant location issue was that the states involved realized they had to get together and cooperate in making these decisions. Pollution is mobile; it doesn't respect political boundaries. One state's gain is often another state's loss—not only in jobs but also in the downstream pollution effects. In this case the states of Alabama, Georgia, South Carolina, Kentucky, North Carolina, Tennessee, Virginia and West Virginia have come together under the name Southern Appalachian Mountains Initiative so that these decisions can be made more rationally on a regional basis without industry playing one state off against another.

This leads me to another, even more difficult air-quality issue in Virginia. The NPS air-quality staff was convinced that a gradual reduction in visibility was taking place in the Shenandoah Valley. Because the vistas from Shenandoah National Park and the Blue Ridge Parkway were being impacted, the Park Service, along with the U.S. Forest Service, actively opposed the state's permitting additional emission sources on the basis that each new source was adding incrementally to the problem. Essentially, the Park Service was saying that the state should not rule on each new permit application but should consider the cumulative impact of a number of new emission sources rumored to be in the planning stages.

This argument really put the Park Service on the cutting edge. Although I could see the thread of truth in our argument, I was bothered by the unfair burden we were putting on Virginia given the fact that

173

much of Virginia's pollution floats in from other states. I was reluctant to restrict Virginia's growth based on other states' transgressions.

The other disturbing point was that the new sources proposed to come on-line in Virginia were expected to be relatively clean, with some of the best air-pollution-control technology in the country. My heart wanted to agree with the NPS air-quality staff position of opposing all new emission sources. But my mind told me that Virginia and other states ought to be ridding themselves of older, more troublesome polluters while permitting new, cleaner sources. If the Park Service were perceived to be against all economic activity we would lose our chance to influence public policy.

With the clean-coal interests in Virginia making very strong and technically correct arguments and with pressure from local communities that needed the power and the jobs, things got more than a little tense in the halls of Interior. They weren't improved when one of our superintendents—pushed and pulled by the air-quality staff to get involved—went way beyond his authority in protesting state air-quality permits.

The assistant secretary for Fish and Wildlife and Parks has the authority to protest such actions, not each individual park superintendent. I'm sure the superintendent was fighting to protect his park and I respected that, but I knew and he knew that he was off the reservation from a legal standpoint. His involvement without the approval of the NPS regional office in Philadelphia or the Washington office had high Interior officials calling for his head. Just about the time I thought the situation was calming down, a new permit application would be filed, the superintendent would get in another fight in the media, and we would start the whole process again.

We did manage some successes, although we didn't get complete victory. The compromise position of getting the new plants to relocate and to retire older, more polluting sources in exchange for new permits was a victory. This approach appears to have merit as this argument continues to brew in Virginia. Again, I think the regional approach has to be taken or states in the downstream pollution channel will have to pay for the sins of their westerly neighbors.

21

The Great Smoky Mountains National Park

One of the most heavily visited national parks, Great Smoky brings more than 9 million tourists to Tennessee and North Carolina each year. The Smokies were authorized for full park development in 1934 when economic times were tough in the country and especially tough for the hill people who made up the population of this region of the country.

The park was not born without controversy. It could be said that some of those who lived within the authorized boundaries of the park lived so far back in the hills that they had to have daylight piped into them. Many of these people were not interested in having their lands converted to parkland. Some had stronger reason to resist than others. The legendary "hide, seek and run" drama played out between the moonshine makers and the revenuers became part of the life of NPS rangers. I am sure there are stills turning corn to sour mash in the hills of the Smokies to this day. It has become more of a hide-and-seek contest than a source of revenue to the residents but it remains a tradition to be dealt with.

Another serious export problem from the Smokies has been the gallbladders of black bears. There have always been wildlife poaching problems in the park, but the one that is the most galling, pardon the expression, has been the slaughter of the black bear to provide gallbladders to the Orient. The bladders are believed to be a powerful aphrodisiac in some cultures and can bring a poacher up to $100 per bladder. By the time a black bear bladder reaches Asia, it may sell for $1,500. To see these creatures slaughtered for no reason other than to remove the gallbladder is disheartening.

If only the wild hogs in the Smokies were as interesting to poachers as the black bear. The park is literally infested with wild hogs, and anyone who has seen the damage a wild hog can do to a park will testify to the need to search for any method of control possible. In fact, the wild hog, or the domesticated hog that has returned to the wild for one reason or another, is a major problem in parks across the nation. Millions of dollars have been spent trying to gain some semblance of control over this animal and the destruction it causes to the vegetation of the parks. In some parks more species of plants have become endangered because of the wild hog than from the presence of man.

On the positive side, I had the distinct honor of being a litter bearer carrying the first male and female red wolves back into the Smokies as we began our efforts to bring that animal back to life in the hills it had ranged many years ago. I couldn't help but think of how excited the local people and conservation organizations were to see the red wolf coming back to the Smokies while the western states were fighting with all their might to keep the grey wolf out of Yellowstone. Why is there such a great difference in attitude about these two reintroductions? Is it the old cattle-sheep-predator battle or does it go deeper than that? Is it a lifestyle thing that goes beyond rational understanding?

Whatever the reason, I was pleased to see the media and park neighbors out in full force to welcome the red wolf back to the Smokies. I also have a secret wish that the red wolf will develop a healthy appetite for wild pig meat.

NPS regional director Bob Baker, Smokies Superintendent Randy Pope, and others took turns carrying the anesthetized animals. I was surprised at their size. I guess I had expected to see an animal bigger than a fox and about the size of a coyote. When we weighed the animals, before turning them loose in their pens where they would become acclimatized over a period of time, the male weighed more than 70 pounds and the female weighed nearly 57 pounds. That is in the range of the size of a German shepherd. These were not small animals. I could well imagine them taking their place in the predatory chain and thinning out the white-tailed deer herd that was also a threat in many parts of the park.

These wolves, like their western cousins, are wary of humans and it will be the rare visitor who ever sees one. To hear the wolves howl at night will send shivers up some people's spines but the danger to humans is almost nonexistent.

The experimental reintroduction of the red wolf to the Smokies is in its early stages and only time will tell how the experiment turns out. The great lesson I learned was that people cared. Hopefully the experiment will be successful, but more than half the battle was won for me that day as I saw parents bring their youngsters to witness the reintroduction. Lessons of ecosystem management were being taught right there, but the term was never mentioned.

One major source of heartburn from the Smokies came from an old settlement area called Cades Cove. This area had been bought and paid for by the government as a part of the creation of the park. As a part of the buyout, some of the owners were given life tenancy with the idea that the properties would gradually be vacated and the area returned to its natural state. The problem was that many of these people didn't want to honor their original agreements. They wanted to find ways to keep passing this property on to the next generation.

I could see why they wanted to do that. These places make great mountain vacation cabins and they offer the advantages of having park property all around them to provide an ambiance that anyone would want to cling to. The problem is that these lands no longer belong to the people who inhabit them—they belong to the people of the United States. We paid for them with the tax dollars of our parents and grandparents. I could not justify allowing these people to continue to exclusively occupy these cabins and retreats that belonged to all of us.

Many—not all—of the people who claimed ownership to these retreats are people of some wealth from Knoxville and they have formed alliances to advance their interests in staying on the land. They are not bad people; they just don't want to give up the lifestyle afforded by the mountain retreats to which they have become accustomed. They have connections to members of Congress and congressional staff who listen attentively to their pleas. They can make the NPS sound like a terrible organization that is depriving them of their fundamental property rights. Don't believe it. If they have a right to those retreats, so do you. You and your parents paid for them.

22

May I Take Your Reservation?

A lot has been written on overcrowding in the national parks. There is no doubt that some parks are overcrowded on some days of the year. Those present there and then are unlikely to be consoled by the fact that the parks are not overcrowded on average. On average, the man standing with one foot on ice and the other on a bed of hot coals should feel okay, but in reality he is pretty uncomfortable.

Much, too, is made of the problem of overcrowding in Yosemite. Certainly Yosemite is nationally—even internationally—one of the most treasured places to visit in the United States. Yosemite always seems to get the most media attention when the subject of overcrowding comes up, but there are other parks that face much the same problem. Grand Canyon and Yellowstone are prime examples. The surprising attendance at Ellis Island has given meaning to overcrowded park facilities in the East.

When people say that Yosemite is overcrowded, they are referring to the impact of mankind on the valley, which is seven square miles and is less than 7 percent of the total acreage of the park. (Yosemite National Park covers 1,169 square miles.) If you insist on going to Yosemite Valley at peak times you will most definitely feel that you are in an overcrowded park. But even on the most crowded days in the valley, there are places elsewhere in Yosemite where you can explore and run little risk of seeing another human being.

Major attractions such as El Capitan, Half Dome and Bridal Falls bring people to Yosemite from all over the world. Longtime Yosemite visitors have learned to go to other, less-visited parts of the park for a more rewarding, natural experience.

On occasion I've spent the night in Yosemite Valley and found it noisier than my condo near the Iwo Jima Memorial in Arlington, Virginia. Those tour buses fire up early as they hurry out of the valley to see the next great attraction on the itinerary.

Thinking of the tour buses at Yosemite reminds me of an occasion in New York City while I was director. I had gone there to help kick off a campaign called The Great American Clean Up, a promotion to encourage people to take better care of our parks. It was cosponsored by the National Park Foundation and the Drackett Company and was a good example of the many partnership programs the Park Service entered into during my tenure.

All those involved gathered at the Plaza Hotel early in the morning for a light breakfast and a discussion of what was to take place during the ceremony. I met a number of people including a handsome guy who said his name was Corbin Bernsen. In an awkward moment of silence I asked Corbin what he did for a living. He replied, "I'm an actor."

I assumed he must be a Broadway actor since we were near Broadway, and I wondered if he knew much about the parks. But he launched into stories of his many hiking and camping trips into Yosemite and how much fun he had wandering the great California parks. He told about arriving in Yosemite Valley late one Friday night and getting confused about the location of his campsite. Not wanting to disturb others, he threw his sleeping bag out on the ground and turned in for the night. The next morning he awoke to the roar of engines and the smell of diesel smoke—he had camped next to the parking lot for the tour buses.

Neither my wife nor I spends much time watching television, so I was unaware that Corbin was a star of "L.A. Law" until he told me. I hated to admit that I had never seen the show, especially since Corbin is such a supporter of the parks. Later that day, back in the office in Washington, I told the ladies at the switchboard that I had met a nice guy who said he was on "L.A. Law" but that I couldn't think of his name. They asked me to describe him and then went into an immediate swoon as they quickly guessed it was Corbin. They couldn't imagine him sleeping next to the tour buses in Yosemite!

The day will come when we will have to make reservations for day use of some of our great parks. The Park Service can control the amount of night use by deciding how many overnight accommodations will be allowed in the parks. It's not the night use that bothers me—it's the day use.

The thousands who jam into Yosemite Valley during the day are the crowds that the media should worry about. Starting a reservation system for day use will not be easy or pleasant. Can you imagine shutting the gate in the face of a family of four who started their trip from New York not knowing exactly when they would arrive at Yosemite? I can see it now: "We've driven two thousand miles to see this place and we only have one day to see it! Throw someone out and let us in!"

The idea of a day-use reservation system shouldn't be that foreign to us. After all, most of us are used to making reservations to go out to dinner or to a play. We buy our tickets ahead of time to go to a ball game.

One major problem is the logistics of setting up a reservation system. The Park Service has not had great luck with its campground reservation program. It would appear to be a simple task, especially in these days of computer communications, but for some reason it has not worked as well as you would think. The campground reservation program is run by a private contractor, as it doesn't make sense to burden our limited park staff with this responsibility. Unfortunately, the contractor tends to hire employees who don't stay around long enough to become familiar with the product—the parks. I called the reservations number just to see how informed the clerks were in offering suggestions and alternatives. Maybe I caught an employee on a bad day, but my impression was that he was poorly oriented to the parks and the range of opportunities for camping. It would be nice to be able to call one 800 number and get information about camping at all federal sites, not just the national parks, but the private sector has yet to tackle that task.

One idea that might make sense is to place the computers and switchboards in a few of the lower-risk federal corrections facilities and train the prisoners to operate the system. You would have a better idea of what the staff turnover rate would be, and the training and work experience would be good for the inmates. There might be a concern about allowing them access to the telephones, but I'm sure some technical genius could figure out a way to solve that problem.

At Yosemite, traffic—especially the automobile—is a major problem in the valley. Sometimes it seems as though people are driving around and around just looking for a place to park. There is a definite need for some sort of an alternative transportation plan. Some people argue that providing more tour and shuttle buses to bring people into the valley while forcing passenger cars to park elsewhere is the answer. I'm not sure I follow their logic. While I am in sympathy with the idea of banning cars in the valley, I am not ready to endorse buses as the answer to the problem. If bumper-to-bumper cars jam the roads in the valley, we can assume the cars will not average more than four occupants per car. With a no-car policy and bumper-to-bumper buses, the number of individuals in the valley would greatly increase. Simple math will show that buses averaging forty passengers per bus will crowd the valley faster than cars. I resisted cries from the tour-bus operators to kick their automotive competition out of the valley.

There must be a creative way to bring people to Yosemite safely and with minimal impact on the environment. Personally, I think day use will have to be curtailed during peak times and that a totally new transportation system will have to be devised. This issue has been and will continue to be studied. Innovative ideas such as the possible use of light rail need to be explored. As new technology becomes available the NPS should be ready to adopt and adapt creative ideas.

Tour operators make a great deal of money bringing international tourists to our parks. I don't begrudge them this, for tourism is one of the few areas in which we run an international trade surplus. But I do think that the operators and the Park Service have a responsibility to channel more tourism to lesser-known parks.

There are many great sites that go relatively unvisited as the tour operators stick to the same routes they have been selling for years. Some creative marketing on the part of the operators would help. Of course, the concessions people would need to be involved in planning the changes, and Park Service people must be in on the ground floor of the discussion. But we could take a lot of pressure off our most fragile park areas if we did a better job of coordinating tours.

Besides the tour bus controversy, a part of the problem of crowding at Yosemite is internally generated. At the peak season, over 2,835 employees are in the park and become part of the congestion problem. Of that number, approximately 735 are NPS employees and the rest are employees of the concessionaire. Of the 2,835 employees, approximately half work in the valley.

Director Ridenour and friend heading down a very steep trail into the Kern River Valley in Sequoia National Park. We had just gone over the 14,000-foot Mineral King Pass and were headed into the wilderness for a few nights and days of camping and exploring.

Many of these employees do not need to actually be in the valley on a daily basis. For example, there is no reason the NPS employees who are serving mainly an administrative function need to be in the valley. The same is true for people working in the motor pool. My goal was to move as many of these functions out of the valley as soon as possible. This goal has to be a long-range one as the dollars it will take to move all of the infrastructure from the valley to locations less environmentally sensitive will take much debate and time to provide.

183

Moving the headquarters operations of the concessionaire out of the valley also makes sense. With all the convenience of modern communications, there is little reason that many administrative functions of the concessionaire need be in the park at all.

A difficult problem to address lies with the food-service people. One day I decided to knock on doors of concessionaire housing to get a better feel for the kind of hours these people worked. Since I chose mid-morning to start my informal survey, I found my knocking brought many sleepy-looking employees to the doors. I found that some worked late in the dining rooms and were sleeping in. Others had been serving breakfast to early risers and had just gotten off their morning shift and were catching a few winks before heading back to serve the noon lunch crowd.

I don't think all of these people can be relocated away from the valley. They would spend all their time on shuttles going back and forth to work, further aggravating the traffic problem. This is a problem that deserves more thought.

Part Six

Historical & Cultural Monuments
&
Urban Parks

23

Taking Care of the White House

When I learned that the White House was part of the national park system, I was both thrilled and awed. I had no idea what would need to be done there, and I would come to depend heavily on Bob Stanton, the very capable regional director for the Park Service's National Capital Region, and Bob's right-hand man for the White House, Jim McDaniel. The discovery that I would chair the Committee to Preserve the White House caused me no small amount of anxiety, and I tried to learn as much about the place as I could.

At the time, the White House was being prepared for painting and sections of its outside walls were covered from public view by huge sheets of canvas. This obtrusive work went on during the entire four years President and Mrs. Bush lived there, and continues today. I'm sure it was disruptive, but there was never a complaint from the president or the first lady.

For the entire four years of our time in Washington, the NPS was involved in fixing and sprucing up the White House for its 200th birthday. A lot may be learned about this country by studying the White House and the people who have occupied it.

In some areas more than forty coats of old paint were removed. When the workers got down to the bare stone, they found scorch marks from where the British had burned the house in 1814. It was sobering to look at the bare stone and the scorch marks and realize than no one had seen these remnants of the nation's early history since they had been painted over after the British invasion. Some of the scorch marks will be left exposed as reminders of this history. I'm sure the Park Service will skillfully weave in the story of Dolley Madison rushing around in time to save the valuable Gilbert Stuart painting of George Washington before she escaped. She also managed to save the portrait of herself that now hangs in the beautiful Red Room.

The White House continues to suffer wear and tear, being the only head of state's home in the world regularly open for public tours. Nearly 1.5 million visitors trek through the house every year. The Committee to Preserve the White House is a group of experts charged to select the colors, paints, wallpapers, curtains, upholstery fabric, carpets, and other such things when replacements are needed. It was a very impressive collection of extremely knowledgeable people—except for me.

Jim Ridenour, speaking at the 200th anniversary celebration of the White House.

While I was no expert on the substance of the discussions, I did know how to chair a meeting and push for consensus. I was less nervous after my first committee meeting, as everyone seemed to get along well. The head of the household staff, Chief Usher Gary Walters, attended all meetings as did Rex Scouten, former chief usher and now curator of the White House. Mrs. Bush was always represented by Susan Porter Rose, her chief of staff.

188

Occasionally we met with Mrs. Bush to discuss what we were doing. One afternoon we went up to the family quarters for tea. It was delightful. Mrs. Bush took us on a tour and showed us some of the special things that were there. A manuscript of President Lincoln's Gettysburg Address—one of five copies he made—occupied a well-protected corner of the Lincoln Bedroom. I felt as though history's hand was on my shoulder as I read it. Mrs. Bush gathered us for tea, and we chatted as she knitted, her dog Millie at her feet. She was very comfortable with herself and with us; I could feel the warmth of her personality in that room.

Our committee moved from room to room deciding what would need to be replaced and when. This was not something we were doing for President and Mrs. Bush; this was taking care of the nation's most historic house for all its people. Tax dollars would not be required, for it was expected that donations would cover the costs. It was an exciting experience to be part of this activity.

I remember our discussions in one room quite vividly. It was the oval Blue Room. We were choosing colors for carpets, walls and draperies, and any one major change would have a lot to do with subsequent choices. As I stood back and listened to the experts debate one choice over another, a consensus appeared to be growing to dramatically change the dominant color pattern. I began to sense that there wasn't going to be much blue in the Blue Room—it would no longer have the unmistakable identity of the Green Room and the Red Room. If they continued their pattern of choices I was afraid the Blue Room would have to be renamed.

I couldn't take it any longer. I blurted out that the public had come to expect blue in the Blue Room. "But blues fight so!" said J. Carter Brown, the much-admired director of the National Gallery of Art. The way he said it caused us all to chuckle—even Carter. But my layman's reaction brought us back on track, and unless someone on the current committee overrides the master plan we set out, there will still be plenty of blue in the Blue Room.

The White House is unique in many ways. Many visitors to Washington, especially international visitors, do not realize they can tour the president's home. It is a tour rich in history and tradition and can be a highlight of any visit.

The National Park Service, in conjunction with the White House staff and the Secret Service, has always done an outstanding job of accommodating those who want to visit the White House, but visitors long toured under conditions that cried out for improvement. If you drove by the Ellipse in the morning—whether it was hot, cold, raining, or snowing—you would see long lines patiently waiting to go through the gates. The restroom situation was deplorable, with no access for the disabled. As a result, there was a variety of portable toilet facilities on the Ellipse—not a great visual starting point for the tour to follow.

Jim McDaniel, the outstanding Park Service liaison to the White House, asked me to drop by to get a better understanding of the rigors a visitor had to go through on the way to the tour of a lifetime. It didn't take much to convince me that we needed a visitor center and we needed it fast. The Park Service had built beautiful visitor centers at other park sites across the country but was woefully deficient at one of our most visited and treasured buildings.

When you have an idea that has something to do with the White House, you need to mount a massive effort to coordinate the interests of many different agencies. It seems that about everyone in town wants to have something to say about anything to be done there, whether it's a minor remodeling, a horseshoe pit or a jogging track.

With Jim's patient persuasion and with the help of Chief Usher Gary Walters, we finally convinced the executive branch agencies that something needed to be done. Mrs. Bush was on our side and made suggestions from time to time about things we might do to make visitors more comfortable. But with the economic climate as it was, it seemed highly unlikely we could get Congress to fund a major project. Besides, those on the president's staff were reluctant to ask Congress for money for the White House. They felt that if you asked for a favor, you had to be prepared to do a favor.

My argument was that we weren't asking for a favor for President Bush, we were trying to relieve the inconvenience of the millions who tour the White House. We wouldn't have been shy about asking for money for Yellowstone or Yosemite. Why should we be shy about the White House?

I asked Congress to help us remodel a part of the Commerce Department building on the corner of 15th Street and Pennsylvania Avenue for a "temporary" visitor facility and construct a small building on the Ellipse to coordinate the tours, offer refreshments and provide access to a better restroom situation. I couldn't believe it when the House and Senate finance committees didn't approve our request. In the context of the Park Service construction budget we were asking for peanuts. Some of those same members of Congress were quite willing to start construction projects in parks back in their states and districts that cost a lot more. As I've mentioned in previous chapters, Congress added projects to our budget that we didn't even ask for.

What to do? My plan was to get several members of Congress to give up a little money that was scheduled for their districts so that we could proceed with the modifications. I needed a champion among them, and Congressman Ralph Regula from Ohio seemed like the right choice. One of the senior Republicans on the Appropriations Committee, he is a determined man and a great lover of the parks.

First I wanted to have Ralph see the actual situation the White House visitor faces. Ralph agreed to make the inspection, especially when I leaned on the point that his office gives out passes to thousands of Ohio constituents who take the tour each year. Convincing Ralph wasn't hard, but convincing members of Ralph's staff that it was a good idea for him to be the first to give a little blood as an example for other members was much tougher. After all, it was congressional staff who had submarined this idea in the first place.

Ralph led the charge on the House side, not without opposition from the powerful chairman of the Appropriations Committee's subcommittee on Interior Department appropriations, Congressman Sid Yates of Illinois. I never knew whether Sid was actually against the project or just didn't want to be for something that Ralph thought was a good idea.

On the Senate side, Senator Don Nickles of Oklahoma was friendly to our cause, but there wasn't much Park Service money headed toward his state. We needed a friendly senator whose state was receiving substantial Park Service funding, and we needed to show how some of that money could be spared for the White House visitor center. A thorough

191

review by our planning an d engineering experts identified Senator Mark Hatfield of Oregon as the best choice.

We had a big project underway at Crater Lake National Park and engineering decisions had been made that would reduce its cost. Senator Hatfield turned out to be pretty friendly to our idea, but he wanted something in exchange for the approximately $700,000 dollars he was agreeing to give up. (It often happens this way in Washington.) We found that he had an unusually strong interest in President Herbert Hoover. What a coincidence that Hoover served previously as secretary of commerce and the Commerce Department building bore his name! The senator wanted a generous display on Hoover's importance both as commerce secretary and as president. He didn't mean some sort of a slide show or a temporary exhibit, he emphasized, but something that stood out and would withstand the test of time.

As I left the Park Service, the planning and engineering was well underway on a visitor center that would serve to tell the story of the White House, distribute the tickets for the tours, and provide a welcome shelter and restroom for visitors before their trek to the White House. Needless to say, Herbert Hoover will be prominently featured. I was just glad Ralph Regula didn't have the same interest in all of Ohio's presidents! In reality, I'm sure the Park Service will give a balanced presentation of the presidents and their lives and times at the White House. I'm also sure the most-asked question of the tour—"Where are the nearest restrooms?"—will at last be satisfactorily answered.

24

Parks, Monuments & Malls–Our Nation's Capital

There is little doubt in my mind: The toughest regional office to run on a daily basis in the NPS is the National Capital Region. Almost anything you can imagine can happen in the capital region and does.

In addition to having the responsibility for such sites as the Lincoln, Jefferson and Vietnam Veterans Memorials, the Washington Monument and the Kennedy Center, this region also has responsibility for more than sixty-seven thousand acres of parks in the Washington, D.C., area as well as patrol and upkeep responsibility for the George Washington, the Rock Creek and the Clara Barton parkways.

The National Capital Region maintains the White House as well as the mall that stretches from the Capitol to the Lincoln Memorial. Rangers will tell you that most anything that is green and looks mowed in D.C. is probably taken care of by the NPS.

Indeed, one D.C. councilman told me that he sometimes gets calls in the night complaining about drug dealing or a fight or something going on in a park. He had a unique way of figuring out who had jurisdiction over the park. He would ask the caller to look and see if the grass had been mowed recently. If the answer was yes, the councilman would call the NPS Park Police. If the answer was no, the councilman figured it was probably a park under D.C. jurisdiction and he would call the D.C. police. This is not a perfect way to tell the difference but it usually worked for the councilman.

I had already been in Washington for a few months when my wife completed her teaching assignment in Indiana and came to join me. We stopped in the headquarters of the Park Police and were met by a young officer who was about to start a routine tour of the area called Hain's Point. Hain's Point consists of open play areas and a golf course surrounded by water on three sides. It is a favorite gathering spot for Washington residents looking for a cool breeze on those hot and humid summer days.

The officer asked if we would like to join him on a short drive around the point to see what goes on during a routine patrol. It sounded innocent enough—something that a Park Service director should do—so we climbed into the back of his patrol car and off we went. Despite the 90-degree heat, I noticed a number of people were wearing long coats. I couldn't figure out why anyone would need a coat on a day as warm as this. The officer replied, "That's to hide the guns they're carrying." My wife and I looked at each other as if to say, What have we gotten ourselves into?

I noticed that the road was one way, and there were two cars ahead of us blocking our passage and two behind us. This seemed rather suspicious and I asked the officer if this was a significant worry to him. He said, "No, they're just making sure we can't go anyplace in a hurry. There are probably drug deals going down in front of us and behind us and those cars are sealing us off from doing much about it. That's one of the reasons we often use horses for patrol."

By now, the officer had my complete attention. He upped the level of anxiety when he slammed on his brakes, jumped out of the car, grabbed a fellow along the street, slammed him up against a car, and started to search him. There were a lot of people in long coats watching all of this and looking in the window at us. I couldn't believe this—we were going to get shot on my wife's first day in the city.

The officer finished his search and climbed back in the car. "What was all that about?" I asked, my heart in my mouth. "I thought I saw that guy dealing crack so I shook him down but didn't come up with the evidence. He probably threw it in the river," the officer calmly replied. "Weren't you afraid you might get shot?" I asked. "Naw, they wouldn't shoot a policeman down here. It would set off a big fuss and we would close this park down. They need this place to do business, and besides, I have a bulletproof vest on." It was all I could do to keep from pointing out that neither my wife nor I had a bulletproof vest on, and I figured if they shot the officer they surely would be interested in eliminating any witnesses.

Crystal Gayle & Jim Ridenour
The National Park Service is the host for the nation's official 4th of July ceremonies. As the official host, I took the opportunity to invite Crystal to provide the entertainment on the Mall. Crystal and I share the same hometown, Wabash, Indiana, so I decided to send Mayor Dallas Winchester and all of Wabash an invitation to the nation's celebration. I was in hopes that 10 to 12 people might actually come. I was thrilled when more than 200 made the 1,200-mile roundtrip. Most came in buses and drove all night. Many were elderly and had never seen the nation's capital. I was delighted they got the chance.

It is my understanding that the Park Police have Hain's Point under better control now than in those days, but I would still urge a tourist to talk with a Park Police officer about the advisability of spending the day at Hain's Point.

In addition to the park property in close proximity to downtown Washington, the National Capital Region has responsibility for many nearby parks such as Great Falls, Manassas, Antietam and other historic areas such as the Frederick Douglass home. The amount of acreage administered may be small in comparison with other NPS regions, but when you consider all of the monuments and memorials to this nation's history and culture the capital region is a storehouse of our most treasured park sites.

Consider this: We lost more than 56,000 men and women in the Vietnam years. Yet we had more than 22,000 casualties on the battlefields at Antietam in one day. It is a shocking statistic. If you want to see a stirring sight, visit Antietam's candlelight ceremony where a candle burns for every casualty on the battlefield of that bloody day. As far as you can see across the battlefield the candles will be glowing. It is a sobering and awesome sight. It never failed to move me to pray that we will never again experience war like that.

Not only does the NPS have the job of caring for all these parks, it also has the job of being the permitting and policing agency for everything that takes place on these properties. As you can imagine, everyone worth their salt who wants to hold a demonstration wants to hold it in a prominent place such as across the street from the White House in Lafayette Park, or on the Mall, or somewhere where the television cameras are sure to find and film them.

The struggle over giving out permits is an everyday battle. Those who apply are sure that their cause is more important than any other cause and they often are irate if they are turned down. Actually, very few are turned down as there are constitutional rights to free speech and the right to assemble that give us all our place in the sun—and a place on the Mall. The number of permits given to assemble, demonstrate or celebrate on NPS property during a year's time runs to approximately 4,000.

A major problem is that all the gatherings collectively put a great deal of wear and tear on the grounds, facilities and staff of the capital region. Things go remarkably well, but when 400,000 people are on the Mall for the average Fourth of July festivities, there will be problems. The sheer numbers of visitors will guarantee a few heart attacks, family squabbles, lost children, an occasional fight—and a big sigh of relief if nothing more serious occurs.

In a town that is already struggling with a major crime problem, the problems intensify in exponential fashion when you mix in a huge tourist population with those living locally. It is to the credit of the National Park Police that things go as well as they do. The National Park Police may well be the best-trained riot-control police force in the world. They are taught and drilled on demonstration-control practices day after day after day.

Those who apply for permits for a demonstration on the Mall usually have a point they are trying to make. They want to get on television and influence voters, the president and members of Congress. The numbers game or the crowd estimating game becomes a big deal to them. For example, all hell breaks loose if the NPS estimates that the crowd that shows up supporting a pro-choice position is estimated to be a larger number than the crowd that shows up taking the opposite position. I am not talking about friendly disagreements on crowd numbers—I am talking about major battles accusing the NPS of manipulating the numbers for political purposes.

First Car—Jim Ridenour and wife Ann; second car—Larry King. Here we are in a 4th of July parade down Constitution Avenue. There was a ceremonial side to being Director of NPS that I hadn't expected. While it was nice to hear the cheers, we knew we were accepting the warmth from the crowd for the National Park Service.

I have seen situations where a congressman will say something like, "There must have been at least a million people on the mall supporting my position on abortion," and then be outraged when the NPS estimates don't agree with his. To protect itself, the NPS has a pretty good system using sample areas and aerial photography to come up with the figures. They don't just stand on the steps of the Lincoln Memorial and count, "One, two, three." A lot of sophisticated math and sampling technology is used in these estimates. No matter how good the sampling technique is there are still a lot of "My dog is bigger than yours," arguments after every major demonstration.

And there are always people looking for a way to make a dollar on the Mall. It bothers me that some of our most sacred areas and moments of reflection can be disturbed by people looking for a way to turn a buck on the tourist. Selling souvenirs is one thing—playing on the grief of a family visiting the Vietnam Wall is another. I know all the legal language that gives people the right to set up tents and peddle one thing or another, but I am ashamed of how some of my fellow Vietnam vets have exploited this situation. Most of them are sincere and are not out to take advantage of anybody—and they must stay a certain distance away from the memorial—but I guess I want the dignity of the memorial kept intact, and it bothers me to see the carnival atmosphere that sometimes exists in the area.

Ours is one of the most beautiful capital cities in the world but it is not without its problems. The safety and enjoyment of tourist and resident alike are often in the hands of the NPS. I think the agency does a pretty remarkable job given the responsibility it has. My hat goes off to the men and women of the National Capital Region.

25

Quayle In the Parks

Vice President Dan Quayle and his family were frequent park visitors. As an agency director I was very happy to have elected officials visit the parks, for it gave us a firsthand chance to tell them of our needs. Of course we wouldn't lobby the vice president, but from time to time a ranger might point out a thing or two that needed attention along the trail.

The Secret Service keeps the movement of the vice president on a "need to know" basis, and he and his family probably made more park visits than I was aware of. I know that the Quayle family made two raft trips on the Colorado River through the Grand Canyon, which they thoroughly enjoyed. There is so little time our top elected officials can spend with their families, and I was proud that they chose our national parks to get in some quality family time.

On the second trip down the Colorado, Marilyn Quayle went over the side at Lava Falls. This is a pretty rough and wild stretch of the river. The Secret Service was quick to spread the rumor that one of theirs had saved her. From what I hear, our Park Service river rats were the true heroes. Maybe the Secret Service had a better publicist!

One story that bugged me and was of some concern to the vice president was about stables for horses at Manassas National Battlefield Park, one of our Civil War areas outside Washington, D.C. The story goes that the vice president and his family were frequent riders at Manassas and that there weren't enough stables to properly care for the nine or ten horses that were kept there. It was said that the vice president wanted me to build additional stables to take care of his needs.

This story got a lot of press. If you didn't have the press you couldn't make a mountain out of a molehill, and that is certainly what happened in this case. Even Congress got involved. Congressman Sid Yates was determined that we shouldn't build more stables, and Senator Dale Bumpers inserted legislative language forbidding us to do so. You can't believe all the power that was brought to bear on this $30,000 to $40,000 decision. I had fights with the superintendent, the regional director, the press, and even Secretary Lujan, who thought the horses should be protected in a small addition to the existing stables.

There is no doubt that Mrs. Quayle and some of the children liked to ride in the park. But the vice president was an infrequent visitor, and there was absolutely no truth to the rumor that he pressured me to build more stables.

The vice president didn't make any specific suggestions but asked me if I were going to build additional stalls based on his need. I assured him that the pressure wasn't coming from him but noted that some of his Secret Service people were friendly with our stable manager and that they were probably fueling the fire. He said he would get that stopped right away. I could tell that he would rather we not build additional stalls because he would be the one to catch the negative publicity.

Personally, I never saw such a big deal made over nothing. After all, when we elect a president and a vice president do we intend for them to go into their houses and never come out?

The true story is that there were certain Civil War history buffs who objected to any horses being at Manassas. Somehow they thought that it was a sacrilege that horses were being ridden on the park's trails and they saw a chance to bring the subject to a boil by linking the vice president's name to this scandalous activity. I wonder what they thought the Union and Confederate cavalries were riding all over the battlefield— elephants?

When you have large, open spaces near major metropolitan areas, as a park executive you have to exercise some common sense. You can't adopt a "stay off the grass" philosophy and expect to make it stick. There are going to be picnickers, Frisbee throwers, hikers and bird-watchers. At a park like Manassas with a tradition of horseback riding in a state known for its love affair with horses, you are going to have to use common sense and look for the compromise that can serve as many interests as possible. I guarantee that a common-sense decision at Manassas would include horses.

26

A Hearing In Woodstock

The Rockefeller family has had a love affair with the parks and a long history of working to protect and preserve them. It has donated large parts of many of our finest assets, including Acadia, Grand Teton, Great Smoky Mountains, and Virgin Islands national parks.

During my four years as Park Service director I had very gratifying relations with Laurance and David Rockefeller and their wives, Mary and Peggy. I found both couples dedicated to preserving and protecting great areas and features of our country and considered it a great privilege to work with them.

Years ago my wife and I were exploring New England on vacation. We stopped to look around the beautiful village of Woodstock, Vermont. If ever I had a vision of New England, this was it. Lots of beautiful old homes on tree-shaded streets, and even a playful, bubbling brook running through the town. In taking a walk to look at the Ottauquechee River and the old iron bridge across it, we noticed a lovely old home sitting on a commanding location overlooking a picturesque valley farm. The home had such a look of quiet dignity that we wondered who in the world might live there.

Imagine my surprise just a few short years later sitting in that home by a roaring fire with Laurance and Mary Rockefeller and discussing the future of that home and surrounding lands. It was Mrs. Rockefeller's inheritance but it had a distinguished history even before her grandfather, Frederick Billings, had purchased it. It had been the home of George Perkins Marsh, for which the Interior Department made it a national historic landmark in 1967 in a ceremony attended by Lady Bird Johnson, then first lady.

Marsh is often referred to as the father of the conservation movement in this country. He was a prolific writer and scholar, speaking, writing and reading many languages. He served for years as the U.S. minister to Italy. His book *Man and Nature*, published in 1864, was considered the most authoritative work on conservation in its time.

Mrs. Rockefeller's grandfather, Frederick Billings, had gazed at the Marsh house longingly when walking by it as a boy and reputedly vowed to purchase it. Little did he know the adventures he would have before doing so. He crossed Panama and arrived in San Francisco about the time of the gold rush. Practicing law, not digging gold, was his key to building a small fortune. He dabbled in real estate, became one of the city's civic leaders, and prospered.

Billings nevertheless longed to go back to Vermont and fulfill his childhood dream. He did so, purchasing the Marsh property in 1869. He sought to make the farm model for conservation. Much of the country had been stripped of its trees and erosion was a problem all over New England. Billings restored the home and surrounding lands to a condition beyond what Marsh had ever hoped for. It was Billings who put to practice the textbook theories of George Perkins Marsh.

Skipping a generation, we come to Mary French Rockefeller, whose love of the land and the home equald her grandfather's. The Rockefellers considered the Woodstock home a place to relax and enjoy nature at its best. Both Laurance and Mary enjoyed hiking the land and discussing ways to improve the preservation of the trees and soils through the best agricultural practices. They have been andare true stewards of the land.

I was asked to come to Vermont for a visit. The Rockefellers were in their earl eighties, and I guessed that they wanted to talk of their hopes for the future of the home and land. I was right.

Both Laurance and Mary are gentle people, almost shy in some ways. Although they had spent more than sixty years in the home, there were many in Woodstock who had never seen them.

Mary has the habit of arising early and walking with her dog, returning in time for studying the Bible in a favorite corner of a room where she has studied since her early childhood. I was awake early and she asked if I would like to join her. As I sat listening to her read from the scriptures, years of history seemed to engulf us in that quiet corner. Her voice tired, and she asked if I would read for a while. I couldn't recall such a feeling of peace and relaxation in many years.

We had breakfast in the small eating area near the kitchen. Wes Frye, one of Laurance's chief advisors, was reading *The New York Times* while Laurance was glancing at the *Wall Street Journal*. Wes asked Laurance, "Do you know how to make a small fortune?" Laurance responded, "No, how?" "You start with a big fortune," was Wes' answer.

As we discussed the variety of ways the house and farm might come under the Park Service, it was clear that the Rockefellers wanted to do everything possible to protect the property. They were also very concerned that the community see this possibility in a positive light.

When private land comes under public ownership, the local government no longer receives property taxes on it. Laurance decided he would soften this negative impact on the community by setting up a foundation arrangement to make payments in lieu of taxes for a period of time after the federal government took over the land. There were many such details requiring a great deal of discussion.

There was no national park land in Vermont other than a portion of the Appalachian Trail, and this was a golden opportunity. The Rockefellers would enjoy a life estate on the property and endow it for the future to make sure that it was well taken care of. Secretary Lujan and I visited Vermont again to discuss the possibilities. We decided what pieces of land beyond the house we would need to tell the story of Marsh, Billings, and, in my mind, the Rockefellers' stewardship. Much of the land would be left to a foundation that would protect it from development, while the Park Service would have the house and the immediate surrounding acres to use in telling the story.

With that rough outline as a guide it was decided we should have a town meeting so the people in the community would know what was going on and have a chance to have their say. Many feared the possible generation of more traffic through the town. Others had different concerns.

The evening of the town meeting Laurance, Mary, Senator Jim Jeffords, and I faced a large turnout. I have been in enough public hearings and meetings in my life to have a pretty good sense of the mood in a room. I sensed tension.

Mary wanted to open the meeting with a prayer. With no guile, just honest concern and emotion, she did so. "To those whom you have blessed with so much, Dear Lord, give us the wisdom to know to do the right thing with the home and the lands" were the words that struck me the most.

Here was a couple ready to give millions in home, lands and dollars to the American people, and she was asking the Lord to guide the decision. She was not showboating for the crowd; she was earnestly praying for guidance in her gentle, humble, time-honored way. If there was any hostility in that crowd it melted on the spot. There were tough questions and long discussions, but the tension was gone.

I have been in many tough hearings—hearings where I had to have police protection—and she gently calmed the crowd with prayer. I have thought about that a great deal. With the lawyers and their clients stopping prayer in our public institutions, we are missing a great healer. Mary Rockefeller showed us that night.

27

Fifty Years After Pearl Harbor

December 7, 1991: fifty years after the Japanese had bombed Pearl Harbor. The National Park Service, which has responsibility for the USS Arizona Memorial, joined hands with the Navy for the commemorative activities.

We knew this would be a very emotional event. For many who were there on that day in 1941, this would be their last pilgrimage to the scene. Add fifty years to the age of the youngest seamen at Pearl Harbor and you realize that the youngest of those still alive had to be sixty-seven or sixty-eight. Most were older.

President and Mrs. Bush came and participated in the events. As I talked with President Bush I was thinking to myself that this was the last president we will have who fought in World War II. It was hard to believe that the generation who fought that war was slipping away.

My job was to serve as a host and master of ceremonies for a number of events spread out over three days. More than survivors of Pearl Harbor attended the various functions. Of course, other veterans attended, as did families of those killed in the attack. There was lots of laughter and more than a few tears. The president himself seemed on the edge of a tear or two as he delivered his remarks on the Arizona Memorial.

Author James Michener and his wife Mari attended and were part of the ceremonies. I told him he was the cause of many lost hours of sleep for me over the years. I would get all involved in a book of his and would stay up long past my bedtime.

Our main stage area was covered, but those in the audience were under the sun and in for a good sunburn if they weren't careful. We had an air-conditioned ready room behind the main stage, and I asked the Micheners if they would like to rest there in the trailer before and after his presentation. They joined us off and on over the three days and were delightful company. Among those present was NPS Chief Historian Ed Bearss, a Marine veteran of World War II who had been wounded in the South Pacific. It was fascinating to hear the "war stories" of these men.

Michener's conversation was just as delightful as his writing. He told about how, after the war, he brought his bride home to Pennsylvania to meet his relatives. He didn't know how they might react to his having an Asian wife. His relatives were not unhappy about that, he recalled, but were upset that she was a Democrat. They both got a good laugh from that story.

I witnessed another backstage meeting that was packed with emotion. Senator Daniel Inouye of Hawaii was waiting to come onstage when an elderly Japanese man approached the tent and asked to meet him. It turned out that this fellow had been one of the pilots who dropped bombs on Pearl Harbor. Senator Inouye had a distinguished war record and had lost an arm in the European theater.

Their conversation was in Japanese so all I could understand was the body language. The elderly pilot reached out to touch the empty sleeve of the senator. Words were exchanged but there were long periods of silence. I watched to see if there was a smile or any sign of humor between the two men. There wasn't.

There is a group called the Pearl Harbor Survivors Association. It is an exclusive club. You had to be at Pearl Harbor in uniform on December 7, 1941. You're not eligible if you were stationed elsewhere on the island—you had to be at Pearl.

The story around was that a Japanese pilot who took part in the raid had applied for membership. He met all the criteria. He was at Pearl Harbor on the day and in uniform. This may sound humorous, and it was to many who heard the story, but the emotions still run deep in that association. I think the pilot was quietly turned down.

There will be many fiftieth-anniversary observances over the next few years as we celebrate one victory or another or mourn one loss or another. Big events took place fifty years ago, both in Europe and the Pacific. As the old saying goes, if we don't remember the past we're doomed to repeat it. Such places as the USS Arizona Memorial serve as wonderful places to educate and remind generations to come.

28

Time to Go Home

The four years went by quickly, especially that last year with all the activity of the election. Of course I was pulling for President Bush, but I knew, in my heart, that I wouldn't want to stay in Washington four more years. Privately I had come to the conclusion that two years into a second term would be enough. Too many people have been in Washington too long for their own good and for the good of the country.

My son Matthew, an advocate of privatizing government functions, had an interesting thought after spending a frustrating day banging his head against the bureaucratic walls of EPA. He put it bluntly: "Everyone in Washington ought to get in line and count off by twos, then all the even-numbered people should leave."

My wife had never been happy about going to Washington. We lived in a nice condominium across the Potomac in Arlington, Virginia, near the Iwo Jima Memorial, but it could be a very lonely place, especially when I was on the road. Ann likes to get her hands in the dirt and plant a garden, and she wanted to go home. I kidded her that she probably voted for Perot to get us an early ticket back to Indiana.

After substitute teaching for a while, Ann landed a regular position teaching sixth graders in Arlington and just loved it. If she could have stayed at the school around the clock she would have been happy. As it was, I worked late and she worked late. We met for meals and sleep. The schedule was hectic and the travel tiring—but it was worth it. I had the best job in government, and by government I mean all governments, foreign and domestic. It wasn't like running a regulatory agency and having everyone look at you as if you had a strange disease. I was in charge of our national parks—the best system of parks in the world.

The election changed my six-year plan, and we headed back to Indiana. Someone sent a news article that described me as a pleasant administrator from Indiana who was not a visionary. I generally don't pay much attention to labels, but I do want to respond with my vision of directing the National Park Service. I learned long ago that you can accomplish a great deal if you don't get hung up on who gets the credit. My style is to build consensus, get people working on the same track, and get the job done. I don't spend a lot of time second-guessing myself. Executives rarely have the luxury of having more than 60 percent of the information they would like to have before making a decision. I would never have had the opportunity to direct the National Park Service without a record of making more good decisions than bad during my career. But the point is that the government needs people who aren't afraid to make decisions, even knowing they won't always be right.

When I became Park Service director, I sensed the need for a leader who could build consensus within the Interior Department for the parks. The Reagan years had not been good for the Park Service; the Carter years had been no better. The leadership at Interior during those times was, at best, neutral to the growing crisis in the parks and, at worst, actually hostile. When you think about it, that was a pretty dumb philosophy for those administrations to take. The Park Service has long been the most admired agency of the federal government, according to the Roper polls. It made sense to me that Interior officials should be playing on the popularity of the parks to the American people. Instead, they were busy throwing roadblocks before park projects. No wonder the Park Service became so dominated by the Congress during those years.

I recall talking with some of the departing Reagan people and having them warn me that Park Service staff was not to be trusted. A departing assistant secretary told me, "We never got control of the Park Service during our administration." At the time I wondered how they expected to achieve any measure of control if they started with the philosophy that park people shouldn't be trusted.

This negative attitude toward the Park Service carried into the first two years of the Bush administration. There were enough Reagan carryovers in key staff positions at Interior that old attitudes persisted. I felt that my first job was to turn this negative atmosphere around. It wouldn't do the Park Service any good to have me become a high-profile media personality; the people of this country already liked the Park Service. My job was to get Interior officials to like the Park Service and recognize the value of our parks to the country. If I could accomplish that I felt that I would serve the agency well.

Ann and Jim Ridenour
Wife Ann and I wait for our raft. Soon we will begin a wild and fun ride down the New River in West Virginia.

Some say there are jealousies among Interior's bureaus. There is truth to that. Working for the Park Service is a little more romantic than reclaiming old coal mines. Not that reclaiming old coal mines isn't important, but it just doesn't carry the glamour of being a ranger at Yellowstone or Yosemite. Those jealousies were a source of great frustration to me when they resulted in petty bickering or bureaucratic blocking of Park Service decisions. When the Park Service got positive media attention the bickering seemed to worsen.

This negative attitude toward the Park Service gradually improved over the four years to the point where I felt it was no longer a problem when I left Washington. I couldn't have changed that attitude had I taken the posture of an ideologue. I would have set up the bureau and myself for a big fall and a further downward spiral of the relationship with those in the secretary's office.

To some extent John Turner, director of the Fish and Wildlife Service, suffered from this same problem. We both got a big boost when Mike Hayden, the ex-governor of Kansas, became the assistant secretary for Fish and Wildlife and Parks and our immediate boss. Mike is a no-nonsense kind of guy who went to bat for us when the secretary would hold meetings at the assistant secretarial level. It didn't hurt that Mike had been a governor and had good ties to the White House. He didn't take long to help us clear a path to the secretary, bypassing the worst of the intermediate foot-draggers who were the problem.

As for the criticism that I wasn't a visionary, I would just say that during my tenure we brought the Park Service back into the executive branch, where it belongs; we challenged the power of the concessionaires and won; we successfully negotiated the largest buyout of a concessionaire in the history of the Park Service when we worked out the complicated plan to deliver the Yosemite Park and Curry Company into the hands of the National Park Foundation; we strengthened the science and resource protection element of the Park Service beyond our expectations; with the help of the White House we almost doubled the Reagan administration's last Park Service budget request; we moved into the arena of becoming a demonstration agency for environmental protection; we created the first office of strategic planning in Park Service history; we added a Parks as Classrooms project that will educate our young people on the importance of our parks; and we charted a visionary course for the Park Service of the future through our thorough introspection during the seventy-fifth anniversary year.

In many ways the national parks mirror the nation. We have chosen places that mean a great deal to us to set aside and protect. Not only have we set aside great natural wonders, we have done the same with our historic and cultural treasures.

A listing of the parks is like laying out the skeletal features of our country. Our nation is built on the collective memory represented by our parks. If we need a lesson in the atrocities of Bosnia or other civil wars we don't have to look far. The bloody battlefields of Antietam and Gettysburg serve as stark reminders of the destruction wrought by internal strife. If we need a lesson in how greed can overcome common sense we can study the impact of agricultural excesses and excessive construction on the Everglades of South Florida.

Sometimes I worry about our country. When I last toured Ellis Island I was reminded of the great melting-pot theory we long believed in. Were we ever a melting pot? Are we a melting pot now? As I see one special interest group or another force its rights above the rights of others, I am concerned.

Could a Bosnia happen here? Do we still remember the bitter lessons taught us in the Civil War? If plants and animals can't survive in the parks because of poor environmental conditions, what's happening outside the parks in less-protected areas? The national parks are great classrooms. The lessons are there to be found. Noted Yale historian Robin Winks calls them the 367 branch campuses of the world's largest university.

The lessons to be learned in the national parks are a collection of the memories of this nation. We must not fail to pass the lessons of the parks on to our children.

Appendix 1

James M. Ridenour's Philosophical Thoughts on National Park Service

April 17, 1989

1. Additional units of the national park system should truly be places of national significance.

2. We must continue to pursue a course of stewardship that allows us to conserve and protect these national treasures.

3. Our first responsibility is to make sure that we are properly safeguarding the treasures we now possess.

4. Operating within the bounds of fiscal reality and common sense, we should add appropriate acreage to the national park system.

5. We should continue to explore innovative ways to preserve and protect lands other than fees and simple purchases. Leases and easements are examples of areas to explore. There are many others.

6. As a Nation, we should be moving toward the goal of acquiring parklands close to the people. It is essential that all levels of government work together in a spirit of cooperation in this objective.

   Each opportunity will be unique and should be evaluated on its merit. There are times when federal ownership is warranted; there are times when state or local ownership makes more sense. There may be times when combinations, including the private sector or foundations, make sense. Outright fee simple federal ownership is not the automatic "correct" answer to our nation's need for more parklands.

7. We have an obligation to be a global leader in our environmental ethic and in resource management in its broadest sense. We must continue to expand our efforts to gather baseline scientific data for use in making the best possible resource management decisions.

8. Just as the world has become a global economy, we are increasingly bound together in our environmental world. It is in our own self-interest that we show, by leadership and example, our strong commitment to environmental protection. We have the ability to influence global thinking on many important environmental issues.

9. We should explore creative ways to work with private groups and individuals to further our goals and objectives in protecting valuable lands. As an example, the Indiana Heritage Protection Campaign has raised $5 million in private funds to be matched by an equal amount of money by the state legislature for the purpose of purchasing and maintaining areas of critical concern to the state. Other states have passed similar legislation.

   I encourage you to identify opportunities to work with foundations and private sources of revenue, both corporations and individuals, that would help us in furthering the goals and objectives of the National Park Service.

10. The Park Service is well-known for its efforts to effectively work with volunteers. Efforts to increase and expand volunteerism should become even more important in our agenda than ever before. People want to help; it is up to us to figure out the best way to utilize the spirit and interest of volunteers.

11. Education, both internal and external, has always been a mainstay in Park Service programs. Our interpretation program enjoys a worldwide reputation for excellence. With President Bush and Secretary Lujan strongly supporting efforts in this area, I urge you to examine our programs with the goal of further strengthening our education commitment.

12. We must strengthen and expand our efforts to recruit and promote women and minorities. This effort should be reflected in our internal education and training programs, and we should encourage external institutions from which we traditionally recruit to strengthen their efforts to recruit, train and provide educational opportunities for women and minorities.

13. Our workforce and the facilities and lands we supervise must be drug free. We must commit to this goal Servicewide and do everything in our power to help battle this scourge that threatens us as a people and a nation.

User Fees

1. User fees are an appropriate method of providing support to the National Park System; however, fees should be appropriate to the services provided and should not prohibit the use of our parks by anyone on the basis of economic status.

2. For those who prefer more costly service, they should expect to pay for the level of service provided. For example, a campsite that has electricity, water and a sanitary sewer hookup, should cost an appropriate amount when compared to a primitive campsite with few amenities.

3. Prices for the use of national park facilities should be kept as reasonable as possible and should not be significantly out of line with comparable services provided in the public sector.

4. The philosophy should be that all are welcome to the park at a minimal cost where entrance fees are charged. Once inside the park, the individual or family may, by choice, opt for services provided at an appropriate cost or may tour and recreate on the lands with little or minor additional financial commitment.

Role of the Concessionaire

1. Concessioner operations play a vital role in Park Service delivery systems. It is doubtful that the Park Service could deliver the level of service that the public demands without the assistance of concession-run operations within the park.

2. I support and encourage the concept of joint government/private arrangements of providing needed service to the public as long as the public is well served and the government receives an appropriate proportion of the revenue stream. It is my philosophy that where appropriate the Park Service should enter into business-like arrangements with the private sector where the public can expect that its government is adequately protected and compensated for the use of public lands by private concessioners.

Land & Water Conservation Fund

1. I have been and remain a supporter of the concept of this fund. It has a proven track record of being one of the best "tools in the bag" to help preserve, conserve and protect our public lands." President Bush has indicated his support of this program to the extent our financial situation will allow, and I believe we will continue to see some form of this program in the future.

2. The concept of comprehensive planning for our recreation and resource needs at all levels of government is as valid today as it has been for many years. I support these planning efforts at all levels of government and would urge the continuation of this program.

Historic Preservation

1. I am a firm supporter of the basic philosophy behind our historic preservation efforts. As a country, we need to be mindful of our past, its inherent natural features and the beauty and culture we have created.

2. I believe the tax incentive program has done more for historic preservation than almost any mechanism I can think of—and it has done it in a way that has created economic momentum in our communities. Much of our country's history and culture would have met the wrecking ball had it not been for this innovative program.

3. I do have a concern that there has been a trend to exclude those not of the "professional historic community" from this program. During my years as state historic preservation officer of Indiana, I witnessed an ever tightening of this maze that complicates the submittal of an application to have a property considered for the National Register of Historic Places.

    Those who hire architects, historians and good lawyers who know the buzzwords that state and federal officials want to hear often get properties on the National Register with few problems. Those without the means to hire consultants sometimes give up in frustration while trying to figure out the tangle of the system.

    I do not want to see these people and the places of historic significance they represent left out of the system and will work to see that it does not happen.

4. Our archeological history cries for survey. On public lands alone we do not have adequate records. Realistically, there is not enough money in our entire budget to properly survey all the lands under public ownership, let alone the lands in private hands. Within the bounds of available funds and common sense, I ask that we add to our base of knowledge whenever and wherever possible and that we preserve and protect those areas and artifacts of value that we find. The sanctity of burial grounds must be respected, and I ask that you work with state and local governments to see that we do our part.

Management Style

1. I am not nor do I intend to become a micro-manager. I expect to work with you as Park Service employees to set the tone and direction, but I fully expect you to carry out the objective once it has been set.

2. I expect short, concise summaries of documents you want to call to my attention.

3. When decisions are to be made, I will expect that alternatives will be researched and presented. I will also ask that you have a recommendation for my consideration.

4. Once I am familiar with our operation and people you may find that I call directly on people in the field for answers to questions from time to time. This is not done to undermine the chain of command, but it is my way of getting at information I need immediately. You may want to ask employees who report to you and who I call or visit to inform you of all that takes place. That is fine with me; my goal is to speed up the process and not set up animosity within your areas.

5. When the public makes inquiries of us, I expect us to be as responsive as possible and in a timely fashion. In order to be as consistent as possible in our responses, I ask that we strengthen the communications links between those responsible for public information in our offices. As soon as I get a feel for the paperwork load, I expect to set a reasonable turnaround time for the answering of inquiries. Even if the answer is going to take considerable time to prepare I find that a short note to the sender indicating we are working on an answer engenders much good will.

6. Once I get settled in, I will increase my travel schedule as much as can be reasonably expected. I fully intend to get out in the field; I know from experience that it is difficult to imagine the full consequences of a problem or opportunity from behind a desk at headquarters.

7. I hope to meet and talk with as many employees as possible in order to get a broad feel for our situation. Let's be serious, but not take ourselves too seriously, and let's enjoy ourselves.

Appendix II: List of National Parks

In the 1970s, 76 National Park units were established by Congress. These were the days sometimes referred to as the Park-of-the-Month-Club," and the action was fast and furious, much of it under the leadership of Congressman Phil Burton of California. while one can question whether all of these units deserved national status, it is hard to question the effective leadership Phil Burton lent to this effort.

[The following list is comprised from information contained in the *National Park Service Almanac* edited & compiled by Ben Moffett & Vickie Carson of the National Park Service Division of Public Affairs—Rocky Mountain Region. Contributing individuals were Terry Hallahan, Linda Griffin, Jan Thresher, Lesta Moffett and Ken Hornback.]

1800s

1. 04/20/32 **Hot Springs National Park**, Arizona.
   (a reservation before Interior Department existed, but not under national park concept. Redesignated as National Park on 08/04/1921.

2. 03/01/72 **Yellowstone National Park,** Wyoming/Montana/ Idaho. World's first National Park

3. 03/02/89 **Casa Grande National Monument**, Arizona (nee Casa Grande Ruin)

4. 09/25/90 **Sequoia National Park**, California

5. 10/01/90 **Yosemite National Park**, California

6. 10/01/90 **Kings Canyon National Park**, California (Nee General Grant National Park); redesignated, enlarged 03/04/1940)

7. 03/02/99 **Mount Rainier National Park**, Washington

1900s

8.	05/22/02	**Crater Lake National Park**, Oregon
9.	07/01/02	**Chickasaw National Recreation Area**, Oklahoma (nee Sulphur Springs Reservation; redesignated Platt National Park 06/29/06; changed 03/17/76, absorbing Arbuckle National Recreation Area.
10.	01/09/03	**Wind Cave National Park**, South Dakota
out	04/27/04	Sullys Hill National Park, North Dakota (nee Sullys Hill Park, separated from system, 03/03/31)
11.	06/26/06	**Mesa Verde National Park**, Colorado
12.	09/21/06	**Devils Tower National Monument** (First National Monument)
13.	12/03/06	**Petrified Forest National Park** (nee National Monument, redesignated National Park 12/09/62)
14.	12/08/06	**Montezuma Castle National Monument**, Arizona
15.	12/08/06	**El Morro National Monument**, Arizona
16.	03/11/07	**Chaco Culture National Historic Park**, New Mexico (nee Chaco Canyon National Monument)
17.	05/06/07	**Lassen Volcanic National Park, California** (as Lassen Peak and Cinder Cone National Monuments, established as National Park 8/9/16)
18.	01/09/08	**Muir woods National Monument**, California
19.	01/16/08	**Pinnacles National Monument**, California
20.	04/16/08	**Natural Bridges National Monument**, Utah
21.	09/15/08	**Kino Missions New Mexico**, Arizona (nee Tumacacori National Monument)
22.	03/20/09	**Navajo National Monument**, Arizona

23. 07/31/09 **Zion National Park**, Utah (nee Mukuntuweap National Monument, enlarged, name changed to Zion National Monument 03/18/18; established as National Park 11/19/19; a second Zion National Monument, proclaimed 01/22/37, incorporated on 07/11/56).

OUT 09/21/09 Shoshone Cavern National Monument, Wyoming, abolished 05/17/54

24. 11/01/09 **Salinas Pueblo Missions National Monument,** New Mexico (nee Gran Quivira National Monument, name changed with addition of two state monuments on 12/19/80).

25. 03/23/10 **Sitka National Historic Park**, Alaska (nee Sitka National Monument, changed 10/18/72)

26. 05/11/10 **Glacier National Park**, Montana

27. 05/30/10 **Rainbow Bridge National Monument**, Utah

OUT 05/16/11 Lewis & Clark Cavern National Monument, Montana, abolished 05/24/37.

28. 05/24/11 **Colorado National Monument**, Colorado

OUT 01/31/14 Papago Saguaro National Monument, Arisona abolished 05/07/30

29. 01/26/15 **Rocky Mountain National Park**, Colorado

30. 10/04/15 **Dinosaur National Monument**, Utah

31. 07/08/16 **Acadia National Park**, Maine (nee Sier de Monts National Monument; became Lafayette National Park 03/26/19; named Acadia National Park 01/19/29).

32. 08/01/16 **Hawaii Volcanoes National Park**, Hawaii

33. 08/09/16 **Capulin Volcano National Monument,** New Mexico, nee Capulin Mountain National Monument

34. 02/26/17 **Denali National Park,** Alaska nee Mount McKinley National Park

35. 08/15/19 **Grand Canyon National Park,** Arizona to National Park Service from United States Forest Service

36. 09/24/18 **Katmai National Park,** Alaska (National Monument until 12/02/80)

37. 12/12/19 **Scotts Bluff National Monument,** Nebraska

38. 12/19/19 **Yucca House National Monument,** Colorado

39. 01/24/23 **Aztec Ruins National Monument,** New Mexico

40. 03/02/23 **Hovenweep National Monument,** Colorado-Utah

41. 05/31/23 **Pipe Spring National Monument,** Arizona

42. 10/15/23 **Carlsbad Caverns National Park,** National Monument, (nee National Monument)

43. 06/08/23 **Bryce Canyon National Park,** Utah, (nee Bryce Canyon National Monument; name changed to Utah National Park 06/07/24; current from 03/25/28.

44. 05/02/24

Craters of the Moon National Monument, Idaho

45. 12/09/24 **Wapatka National Monument,** Arizona

46. 02/26/25 **Glacier Bay National Park,** Alaska (nee National Monument until 12/02/80)

47. 03/03/25 **Mount Rushmore National Monument,** South Dakota

48. 05/22/26 **Shenandoah National Park,** Virginia

49. 05/22/26 **Great Smoky Mountains National Park,** North Carolina-Tennessee

50. 05/25/26 **Mammoth Cave National Park,** Kentucky

51.	02/26/29	**Grand Teton National Park,** Wyoming
52.	03/04/29	**Badlands National Park,** South Dakota, nee National Monument, redesignation 11/10/78
53.	04/12/29	**Arches National Park,** Utah
54.	07/03/30	**Colonial National Historic Park,** Virginia
55.	02/14/31	**Canyon de Chelly National Monument,** Arizona
56.	03/03/31	**Isle Royale National Park,** Michigan
57.	03/30/31	**George Washington Birthplace National Monument,** Virginia
58.	03/17/32	**Great Sand Dunes National Park,** Colorado
ABS	12/22/32	**Grand Canyon National Monument,** Arizona, absorbed by Grand Canyon National Park, 1/3/75
59.	01/18/33	**White Sands National Monument,** New Mexico
60.	02/11/33	**Death Valley National Monument,** Nevada-California
61.	03/02/33	**Black Canyon of the Gunnison National Park,** Colorado
62.	03/02/33	**Morristown National Historic Park,** New Jersey
63.	08/09/33	**National Capital Parks,** District of Columbia, originated as office of National Parks, Buildings & Reservations, in the Department of the Interior. National Capital Parks first used in District of Columbia Appropriations Act of 06/04/34
64.	08/10/33	**Ford's Theatre National Historic Site,** District of Columbia transferred from office of Public Parks of the National Capital as Lincoln Museum, redesignated Ford's Theatre 04/14/65; combined with House Where Lincoln Died (also transferred 08/10/33) ON 06/23/70)

65/68. 08/10/33 **Lincoln Memorial,**
Washington Monument,
White House, District of Columbia
George Washington Memorial Parkway,
Virginia-Maryland, transferred from office of Public
Parks of the National Capital

69/76 08/10/33 **Chichamauga & Chattanooga National**
Monument Park, Georgia-Tennessee,
Fort Donelson National Monument Park, Tn,
Fredericksburg & Spotsylvania County
Battlefields Memorial National Battlefield Park,
Virginia,
Gettysburg National Monument Park, Pa,
Guilford Courthouse National Monument Park,
North Carolina,
Kings Mountain National Monument Park, SC,
Shiloh National Monument Park, Tennessee,
Vicksburg National Monument Park, Mississippi,
from War Department.

77/79. 08/10/33 **Moores Creek National Battlefield,** North Carolina;
Petersburg National Battlefield, Virginia;
Stones River National Battlefield, Tennessee
Initially as National Memorial Park and names
subsequently changed to national battlefields.

80. 08/10/33 **Abraham Lincoln Birthplace National Historic**
Site, Kentucky, from War Department as national
park, changed to National Historic Park 8/11/39, and
to National Historic Site 9/8/59.

81. 08/10/33 **Fort McHenry National Monument and Historic**
Shrine, Maryland from War Department as National
Park. Designation changed 9/11/39.

82.　　08/10/33　**Antietam National Battlefield,** Maryland
From War Department 8/10/33 as National
Battlefield. Redesignated 11/10/78.

83.　　08/10/33　**Appomattox Court House National Historic Park,**
Virginia. As battle site, changed to National Historic
Monument 8/13/35; to current name 4/15/54.

84.　　08/10/33　**Brices Cross Roads National Battle Site,**
Mississippi (MS) from War Department as battle
site.

85.　　08/10/33　**Jean Lafitte National Historic Park and Preserve,**
Lousiana, from War Department as Chalmette
Monument and Grounds, to National Historic Park
8/10/33, absorbed in Jean Lafitte 11/10/78.

86/89.　08/10/33　**Cowpens National Battlefield,** South Carolina;
Fort Necessity National Battlefield, Pennsylvania;
Kennesaw Mountain National Battle Park, Ga.
Tupelo National Battlefield, Mississippi
Transferred from War Department as battle sites.

OUT　　08/10/33　White Plains National Battlefield, New York
From War Department. Removed from National Park
System 5/20/56.

90.　　08/10/33　**Big Hole National Battlefield,** Montana
From War Department as national monument,
changed to national battlefield 5/17/63.

91.　　08/10/33　**Cabrillo National Monument,** California
From War Department 9/10/33.

OUT　　08/10/33　Castle Pinckney National Monument, New York
From War Department and abolished.

OUT　　08/10/33　Father Millet Cross National Monument, New York
From War Department and transferred to state,
9/7/49.

225

92.	08/10/33	**Castillo de San marcos national Monument**, Florida, from War Department as Fort Marion National Monument. Changed 6/5/42.
93.	08/10/33	**Fort Matanzas National Monument**, Florida From War Department
94.	08/10/33	**Fort Pulaski National Monument**, Georgia From War Department
ABS	08/10/33	Meriwether Lewis National Monument, Tennessee-Alabama-Mississippi From War Department, and absorbed by Natchez Trace Parkway.
95.	08/10/33	**Mound City Group National Monument**, Ohio From War Department
96.	08/10/33	**Statue of Liberty National Monument**, New York From War Department
REM	08/10/33	Camp Blount Tablets National Memorial, Tennessee From War Department, and removed from NPS list in 1944.
97.	08/10/33	**Wright Brothers National Memorial**, South Carolina, from War Department as Kill Devil Hill Monument National Memorial; redesignated 12/1/53.
REM	08/10/33	New Echota Marker National Memorial, Georgia From War Department but not activated as NPS area.
98.	08/10/33	**Arlington House, the Robert E. Lee Memorial**, Virginia, from War Department as Lee Mansion Memorial, name changed 6/30/72.
ABS	08/10/33	Battleground National Cemetery, Washington, D.C. From War Department, now a part of National Capital Parks.

ABS   08/10/33   The following national cemeteries: Antietam, Vicksburg, Gettysburg, Chattanooga, Fort Donelson, Shiloh, Fredericksburg
Transferred from War Department and became part of their parks in 1974. Also, Poplar Grove National Cemetery became a part of Petersburg National Memorial Park, Virginia, and Yorktown National Cemetery, became a part of Colonial National Historic Park, Virginia.

99/110   08/10/33   The following from USDA-Forest Service:
Gila Cliff Dwellings National Monument, New Mexico;
Tonto National Monument, Arizona;
Jewel Cave National Monument, South Dakota;
Oregon Caves National Monument, Oregon;
Devils Postpile National Monument, California;
Walnut Canyon National Monument, Arizona;
Bandelier National Monument, New Mexico;
Timpanjogos Cave National Monument, Utah;
Chiricahua National Monument, Arizona;
Lava Beds National Monument, California;
Sunset Crater Volcano National Monument, Az;
Saguaro National Monument, Arizona

111.   08/10/33   **Olympic National Park**, Washington
From Forest Service as Mount Olympus National Monument, renamed as national park 6/29/38.

112.   08/22/33   **Cedar Breaks National Monument**, Utah

113.   05/30/34   **Everglades National Park**, Florida

114.   06/14/34   **Ocmulgee National Monument**, Georgia

115.   06/24/34   **Thomas Jefferson Memorial**, Washington, D.C.

116.   01/04/35   **Dry Tortugas National Park**, Florida

117.   06/20/35   **Big Bend National Park,** Texas

118.   08/21/35   **Fort Sanwix National Monument,** New York

ABS   08/27/35   Ackis Battleground National Monument, Mississippi
                    Into Natchez Trace Parkway 8/10/61.

119.   08/29/35   **Andrew Johnson National Historic Site,** Tennessee
                    As national monument, changed 12/11/63.

120.   12/11/35   **Jefferson National Expansion Memorial National
                    Historic Site,** Missouri

121.   03/02/36   **Richmond National Battle Park,** Virginia

122.   03/19/36   **Homestead National Monument of America,** Neb.

123.   05/26/36   **Fort Frederica National Monument,** Georgia

124.   06/02/36   **Perry's Victory and International Peace
                    Memorial,** Ohio. As national monument. Changed
                    10/26/72.

125.   06/29/36   **Whitman Mission National Historic Site,** Wa.

126.   06/30/36   **Blue Ridge Parkway,** Virginia-North Carolina

127.   08/10/36   **Joshua Tree National Monument,** California

128.   10/13/36   **Lake Mead National Recreation Area,** Nevada-
                    Arizona. Agreement with Bureau of Reclamation for
                    NPS administration of area called Boulder Dam
                    National Recreation Area; name changed 8/11/47.

129.   11/14/36   **Catoctin Mountain Park,** Maryland
                    Transferred from Resettlement Admnistration as
                    recreation demonstration area; name changed
                    7/12/54.

130.   11/14/36   **Prince William Forest Park,** Virginia
                    From Resettlement Administration as recreation
                    demonstration area as Chopawamsic Recreation
                    Demonstration Area; name changed 6/22/48.

131.	04/13/37	**Organ Pipe Cactus national Monument,** Arizona

132.	08/02/37	**Capitol Reed National Park,** Utah

As national monument; to national park 12/18/71.

133.	08/17/37	**Cape Hatteras National Seashore,** North Carolina

134.	08/25/37	**Pipestone National Monument,** Minnesota

135.	03/17/38	**Salem Maritime National Historic Site,** Ma.

136.	05/26/38	**Channel Islands National Park,** California

Was national monument until 3/5/80.

137.	05/18/38	**Natchez Trace Parkway,**

Mississippi-Alabama-Tennessee

138.	06/01/38	**Saratoga National Historic Park,** New York

139.	07/16/38	**Fort Laramie National Historic Site,** Wyoming

140.	08/03/38	**Hopewell Village National Historic Site,** Pa.

141.	05/26/39	**Federal Hall National Memorial,** New York

Memorial historic site until 9/11/55.

142.	07/25/39	**Tuzigoot National Monument,** Arizona

143.	05/05/40	**Manassas National Battlefield Park,** Virginia

144.	06/11/40	**Cumberland Gap National Historic Park,**

Kentucky-Virginia-Tennessee

145.	07/01/40	**Little Bighorn Battlefield National Monument,**

Montana, from War Department as National
Cemetery of Custer's Battlefield Reservation;
changed to Custer Battlefield National Monument
3/22/46; changed to Little Bighorn Battlefield
National Monument 12/10/91.

146.	12/18/40	**Vanderbilt Mansion National Historic Site,** NY.

147.	04/05/41	**Fort Raleigh National Historic Site,** North Carolina

229

148.   08/18/41   **Coronado National Memorial,** Arizona
Was International Memorial; changed 7/9/52.

149.   07/14/53   **George Washington Carver National Monument,** Missouri

150.   01/15/44   **Home of Franklin D. Roosevelt National Historic Site,** New York

151.   06/30/44   **Harpers Ferry National Historic Park,** Maryland-West Virginia. As national monument until 5/29/63.

152.   07/12/46   **Castle Clinton National Monument,** New York

153.   12/09/46   **Adams National Historic Site,** Massachuestts Changed from Adams Mantion National Historic Site 11/5/52.

154.   12/18/46   **Coulee Dam National Recreation Area** Agreement with Bureau of Reclamation, Bureau of Indian Affairs on NPS adminimstration.

155.   05/25/47   **Theodore Roosevelt National Park,** North Dakota From memorial park 11/10/78.

156.   03/11/48   **De Soto National Memorial,** Florida

157.   04/28/48   **Fort Sumter National Monument,** South Carolina Accepted by Department of Interior from Deaprtment of Army 7/12/48

158.   06/19/48   **Fort Vancouver National Historic Site,** Washington

159.   06/22/48   **Hampton National Historic Site,** Maryland

160.   06/22/48   **Independence National Historic Park,** Pennsylvania

161.   02/14/49   **San Juan National Historic Site,** Puerto Rico

162.   06/08/49   **Saint Croix Island International Historic Site** Redesignated from national monument on 9/25/84.

163. 10/25/49 **Effigy Mounds National Historic Site,** Iowa

164. 09/21/50 **Fort Caroline National Memorial,** Florida

165. 09/02/51 **Grand Portage National Monument,** Minnesota

166. 03/04/52 **Christiansted National Historic Site,** Virgin Islands
Changed from Virgin Islands National Historic Site

REM   06/27/52 Shadow Mountain National Recreation Area,
Colorado, to U.S. Department of Agriculture-Forest
Service 10/11/78

167. 06/28/54 **Fort Union National Monument,** New Mexico

168. 07/26/55 **Pu'uhonua o Honaunau National Historic Park,**
Hawaii. Name changed from City of Refuge National
Historic Site 11/10/78.

169. 12/06/55 **Edison National Historic Site,** New Jersey
Edison Laboratory National Monument proclaimed
7/14/56. Combined as National Historic Site 9/5/62.

170. 04/02/56 **Booker T. Washington National Monument,** Va.

171. 07/20/56 **Pea Ridge National Memorial Park ,** Arkansas

172. 07/25/56 **Horseshoe Bend National Memorial Park,** Ala.

173. 08/02/56 **Virgin Islands National Park,** Virgin Islands

174. 04/02/57 **Golden Spike National Historic Site,** Utah

175. 05/29/58 **Fort Clatsop National Memorial,** Oregon

176. 04/18/58 **Glen Canyon National Recreation Area,** Arizona-
Utah. Agreement with Bureau of Reclamation.

177. 08/14/58 **General Grant National Memorial,** New York

178. 08/14/59 **Minute Man National Historic Park,** Ma.

179. 04/22/60 **Wilson's Creek National Battlefield,** Missouri
From National Battlefield Park 12/16/70.

180.	06/03/60	**Bent's Old Fort National Historic Site,** Colorado
181.	06/06/60	**Arkansas Post National Memorial,** Arkansas
182.	09/13/60	**Haleakala National Park,** Hawaii Part of Hawaii National Park since 4/1/16, and redesignated.
183.	01/18/61	**Chesapeake and Ohio Canal National Historic Park,** Washington, D.C.-Maryland-West Virginia
REM	01/19/61	**St. Thomas National Historic Site,** Virgin Islands Ceded to VirginIslands government 2/75.
184.	05/11/61	**Russell Cave National Monument,** Alabama
185.	08/07/61	**Cape Cod National Site,** Massachusetts
186.	09/08/61	**Fort Davis National Historic Site,** Texas
187.	09/13/61	**Fort Smith National Historic Site,** Arkansas
188.	10/04/61	**Piscataway Park, Maryland**
189.	10/28/61	**Buck Island Reef National Monument,** Virgin Isles
190.	02/19/62	**Lincoln Boyhood National Memorial,** Indiana
191.	04/27/62	**Hamilton Grange National Memorial,** New York
192.	07/25/62	**Theodore Roosevelt Birthplace National Historic Site,** New York
193.	07/25/62	**Sagamore Hill National Historic Site,** New York
194.	09/05/62	**Frederick Douglass Home,** Washington, D.C.
195.	09/13/62	**Point Reyes National Site,** California
196.	09/28/62	**Padre Island National Site,** Texas
197.	08/27/64	**Ozark National Scenic Riverways,** Missouri
198.	08/30/64	**Fort Bowie National Historic Site,** Arizona
199.	08/31/64	**Fort Larned National Historic Site,** Kansas

200. 08/11/64 Saint-Gaudens National Historic Site, NH.

201. 08/31/64 Allegheny Portage Railroad National Historic Site, Pennsylvania

202. 08/31/64 Johnstown Flood National Memorial, Pa.

203. 08/31/64 John Muir National Historic Site, California

204. 09/11/64 Fire Island National Site, New York

205. 09/12/64 Canyonlands National Park, Utah

AFF 10/13/64 Ice Age National Scientic Reserve, Wisconsin

206. 12/31/64 Bighorn Canyon National Recreation Area, Wyoming-Montana

ABS 02/01/65 Arbuckle National Recreation Area, Oklahoma Absorbed in Chickasaw National Recreation Area 3/17/76.

207. 02/11/65 Curecanti National Recreation Area, Colorado

208. 03/15/65 Lake Meredith National Recreation Area, Texas Sanford National Recreation Area to 10/16/72.

209. 05/15/65 Nez Perce National Historic Park, Idaho

210. 06/05/65 Agate Fossil Beds National Monument, Nebraska

211. 06/28/65 Pecos National Historical Park, New Mexico Was national monument.

212. 08/12/65 Herbert Hoover National Historic Site, Iowa

213. 08/21/65 Alibates Flint Quarries, Texas

214. 08/28/65 Hubbell Trading Post National Historic Site, Az.

215. 09/01/65 Delaware Water Gap National Recreation Area, Pennsylvania-New Jersey

216. 09/21/65 Assateague Island National Site, Md.-Va.

217. 09/30/65 Pennsylvania Avenue National Historic Site, D.C.

218.	10/22/65	Roger Williams National Memorial, Rhode Island
219.	11/08/65	Whiskeytown-Shasta-Trinity National Recreation Area, California
220.	11/11/65	Amistad National Recreation Area, Texas
221.	03/10/66	Cape Lookout National Site, North Carolina
222.	06/20/66	Fort Union Trading Post National Historic Site, North North Dakota-Montana
223.	06/30/66	Chamizal National Memorial, Texas
224.	07/23/66	George Rogers Clark National Historic Park, In.
225.	09/09/66	San Juan Island National Historic Park, Wa.
226.	10/15/66	Guadalupe Mountains National Park, Texas
227.	10/15/66	Pictured Rocks National Lakeshore, Michigan
228.	10/15/66	Wolf Trap Farm Park for the Performing Arts, Va.
229.	11/02/66	Theodore Roosevelt Inaugural National Historic Site, New York
230.	11/05/66	Indiana Dunes National Lakeshore, Indiana
231.	05/26/67	John F. Kennedy National Historic Site, Ma.
232.	11/27/67	Eisenhower National Historic Site, Pennsylvania
233.	04/05/68	Saugus Iron Works National Historic Site, Ma.
234.	10/02/68	North Cascades National Park, Washington
235.	10/02/68	Lake Cheland National Recreation Area, Wa.
236.	10/02/68	Ross Lake National Recreation Area, Washington
237.	10/02/68	Redwood National Park, California

238.   10/02/68   **Appalachian National Scenic Trail,**
Maine-New Hampshire-Vermont-Massachusetts-
Connecticut-New York-New Jersey-Pennsylvania-
Maryland-Virginia-West Virginia-Tennessee-North
Carolina-Georgia

239.   10/17/68   **Carl Sandburg Home National Historic Site,** NC.

240.   10/18/68   **Biscayne National Park,** Florida. As national
monument, changed to national park 6/28/80.

OUT   01/16/69   **Mar-A-Lago National Historic Site,** Florida
Deauthorized in 1980.

ABS   01/20/69   Marble Canyon National Monument, Arizona
Absorbed in Grand Canyon National Park 1/3/75.

241.   08/20/69   **Florissant Fossil Beds National Monument,** Co.

242.   09/04/69   **St. Croix National Scenic Riverway,** Wisconsin-
Minnesota, under NPS 4/69, authorized 10/2/68.

OUT   09/04/69   **Wolf National Scenic Riverway,** Wisconsin
Removed from system

243.   12/2/69   **William Howard Taft National Historic Site,** Ohio

244.   12/2/69   **Lyndon B. Johnson National Historic Park,** Texas
Changed from National Historic Site on 12/28/80

245.   01/01/70   **Theodore Roosevelt Island,** Washington, D.C.
Transferred from the Office of Public Buildings &
Public Parks of the National Capital on 8/10/33, but
not counted as a separate area until 1/1/70 in
"National Parks and Ladmarks."

246.   09/26/70   **Apostle Islands National Lakeshore,** Wisconsin

247.   10/16/70   **Andersonville National Historic Site,** Georgia

248.   10/16/70   **Fort Point National Historic Site,** California

249.   10/21/70   **Sleeping Bear Dunes National Lakeshore,** Mi.

250.	01/08/71	**Gulf Islands National Site,** Florida-Mississippi
251.	01/08/71	**Voyageurs National Park,** Minnesota
252.	08/18/71	**Lincoln Home National Historic Site,** Illinois
253.	03/01/72	**Buffalo National River,** Arkansas
254.	06/15/72	**John F. Kennedy Center for the Performing Arts,** Washington, D.C. Non-performing arts functions were given to the National Park Service from the Smithsonian; transferred back in 1994.
255.	08/17/72	**Puukohola Heiau National Historic Site,** Hawaii
256.	08/25/72	**John D. Rockefeller Jr. Memorial Parkway,** Wy.
257.	08/25/72	**Grant-Kohrs Ranch National Historic Site,** Mt.
258.	10/09/72	**Longfellow National Historic Site,** Massachusetts
259.	10/21/72	**Hohokam-Pima National Monument,** Arizona
260.	10/21/72	**Thaddeus Kosciuszko National Memorial,** Pa.
261.	10/23/72	**Cumberland Island National Site,** Georgia
262.	10/23/72	**Fossil Butte National Monument,** Wyoming
263.	10/27/72	**Lower St. Croix National Scenic River,** Mn.-Wi.
264.	10/27/72	**Gateway National Recreation Area,** NJ-NY
265.	10/27/72	**Golden Gate National Recreation Area,** California
266.	03/07/74	**Big South Fork National Resource & Recreation Area,** Kentucky-Tennessee
267.	03/07/74	**Boston National Historic Park,** Massachusetts
268.	10/11/74	**Big Cypress National Preserve,** Florida
269.	10/24/74	**Big Thicket National Preserve,** Texas
270.	10/24/74	**John Day Fossil Beds National Monument,** Oregon

271. 10/26/74 **Knife River Indian Villages National Historic Site,** North Dakota

272. 10/26/74 **Martin Van Buren National Historic Site,** New York

273. 10/26/74 **Springfield Armory National Historic Site,** Ma.

274. 10/26/74 **Tuskegee Institute National Historic Site,** Alabama

275. 10/26/74 **Clara Barton National Historic Site,** Maryland

276. 12/27/74 **Cuyahoga Valley National Recreation Area,** Ohio

277. 10/27/74 **Fort Washington Park,** Maryland. Transfer from the War Department authorized 5/29/30, made effective in 1940. Fort Washington not couted as independent until this date in "National Parks & Landmarks."

278. 01/01/75 **National Mall,** Washington, D.C. From the Office of Public Buildings & Public Parks of the National Capital on 8/10/33; first counted in "National Parks and Landmarks" on 1/1/75.

279. 01/01/75 **Rock Creek Park,** Washington, D.C. Transferred from the Office of Public Buildings & Public Parks of the National Capital on 8/10/22; first counted in "National Parks and Landmarks" on 1/1/75.

280. 01/01/75 **Greenbelt Park,** Maryland. From Public Housing Authority on 10/3/50; first counted as area of system on 1/1/75 in "National Parks and Landmarks."

281. 01/01/75 **Lyndon Baines Johnson Memorial Grove on the Potomac,** Washington, D.C. Counted as National Park System unit in "National Parks & Landmarks" on 1/1/75.

282. 01/03/75 **Canaveral National Site,** Florida

283. 06/30/76 **Klondike Gold Rush National Historic Park,** Alaska-Washington

284. 07/04/76 **Valley Forge National Historic Park**, Pennsylvania

285. 08/19/76 **Ninety-Six National Historic Site**, South Carolina

286. 10/12/76 **Obed Wild and Scenic River**, Tennessee

287. 10/18/76 **Congaree Swamp National Monument**, SC.

288. 10/21/76 **Monocacy National Battlefield**, Maryland
From the War Department as a battlefield site on 8/10/33; authorized as National Memorial Park 6/21/34, but not activated until 10/21/76 pending purchase authority.

289. 05/27/77 **Eleanor Roosevelt National Historic Site**, NY

290. 04/17/78 **Constitution Gardens**, Washington, D.C.

291. 06/05/78 **Lowell National Historic Park**, Massachusetts

292. 08/15/78 **Chattahoochee River National Recreation Area**, Georgia.

293. 08/18/78 **War in the Pacific National Historic Park**, Guam

294. 11/10/78 **Santa Monica Mountains National Historic Park**, California

295. 11/10/78 **Kaloko-Honokohau National Historic Park**, Hi.

296. 11/10/78 **Fort Scott National Historic Site**, Kansas

297. 11/10/78 **Thomas Stone National Historic Site**, Maryland

298. 11/10/78 **Delaware National Scenic River**, New York-New Jersey-Pennsylvania

299. 11/10/78 **Upper Delaware Scenic & Recreational River**, New York-Pennsylvania

300. 11/10/78 **Edgar Allan Poe National Historic Site**, Pa.

301. 11/10/78 **Friendship Hill National Historic Site**, Pa.

302. 11/10/78 **Palo Alto Battlefield National Historic Site**, Texas

303.	11/10/78	**Rio Grande Wild and Scenic River,** Texas
304.	11/10/78	**San Antonio Missions National Historic Park,** Tx.
305.	11/10/78	**Maggie L. Walker National Historic Site,** Virginia
306.	11/10/78	**New River Gorge National River,** West Virginia
307.	11/10/78	**Missouri National Recreational River,** Nebraska
AFF.	11/10/78	**Ebey's Landing,** Washington To affiliated area, 1988.
308.	11/10/78	**St. Paul's Church National Hisotirc Site,** New York
309.	12/01/78	**Aniakchak National Monument,** Alaska
310.	12/01/78	**Bering Land Bridge National Preserve,** Alaska Originally designated as a national monument, redesignated as a national preserve on 12/2/80.
311.	12/01/78	**Cape Krusenstern National Monument,** Alaska
312.	12/01/78	**Gates of the Arctic National Park,** Alaska National monument until 12/2/80.
313.	12/01/78	**Kenai Fjords National Park,** Alaska National monument until 12/2/80.
314.	12/01/78	**Kobuk Valley National Park,** Alaska National monument until 12/2/80.
315.	12/01/78	**Lake Clark National Park,** Alaska National monument until 12/2/80.
316.	12/01/78	**Noatak National Preserve,** Alaska National monument until 12/2/80.
317.	12/01/78	**Wrangell-St. Elias National Park,** Alaska National monument until 12/2/80.
318.	12/01/78	**Yukon-Charley National Preserve,** Alaska National monument until 12/2/80.
319.	10/12/79	**Frederick L. Olmstead National Historic Site,** Ma.

320.	07/01/80	**Vietnam Veterans Memorial,** Washington, D.C.
321.	07/29/80	**Eugene O'Neill National Historic Site,** California
REM	09/08/80	Georgia O'Keeffe National Historic Site, New Mexico deauthorized 1983
322.	10/10/80	**Martin Luther King Jr. National Historic Site,** Ga.
323.	10/10/80	**USS Arizona Memorial,** Hawaii Transferred to NPS from U.S. Navy
324.	12/02/80	**Aniakchak National Preserve,** Alaska
325.	12/02/80	**Denali National Preserve,** Alaska
326.	12/02/80	**Gates of the Arctic National Preserve,** Alaska
327.	12/02/80	**Glacier Bay National Preserve,** Alaska
328.	12/02/80	**Katmai National Preserve,** Alaska
329.	12/02/80	**Lake Clark National Preserve,** Alaska
330.	12/02/80	**Wrangell-St. Elias National Preserve,** Alaska
331.	12/02/80	**Alagnak Wild River,** Alaska
332.	12/22/80	**Kalaupapa National Historic Park,** Hawaii
333.	12/28/80	**James A. Garfield National Historic Site,** Ohio
334.	12/28/80	**Women's Rights National Historic Park,** New York
335.	03/23/83	**Harry S Truman National Historic Site,** Missouri
336.	03/28/83	**Natchez Trace National Scenic Trail,** Ga.-Al.-Tn.
337.	03/28/83	**Potomac Heritage National Scenic Traill,** Washington, D.C.-Virginia-Pennsylvania
338.	10/27/86	**Great Basin National Park,** Nevada
339.	12/23/87	**Jimmy Carter National Historic Park,** Georgia
340.	12/31/87	**El Malpais National Monument,** New Mexico
341.	02/16/88	**Timucuan Ecological & Historic Preserve,** Florida

342.   06/27/88   **San Francisco Maritime National Historic Park,** California

343.   09/08/88   **Charles Pinckney National Historic Site,** SC

344.   10/07/88   **Natchez National Historic Park,** Mississippi MS

345.   10/10/80   **Boston African American National Historic Site,** Massachusetts, authorized in 1980, it was added to NPS by director in 1988.

346.   10/26/88   **Bluestone National Scenic River,** West Virginia

347.   10/26/88   **Gauley River National Recreation Area,** WV

348.   10/30/86   **Steamtown National Historic Site,** Pennsylvania *Authorized in 1986 as an affiliated area; changed to NPS unit in 1988.

349.   10/31/88   **Poverty Point National Monument,** Louisiana

350.   10/31/88   **Zuni-Cibola National Historic Park,** New Mexico

351.   10/31/88   **The National Park of American Samoa,** Samoa

352.   11/18/88   **City of Rocks National Reserve,** Idaho

353.   11/18/88   **Hagerman Fossil Beds National Monument,** Idaho

354.   11/18/88   **Mississippi National River and Recreation Area,** Minnesota

355.   10/03/89   **Ulysses S. Grant National Historic Site,** Missouri

356.   06/27/90   **Petroglyph National Monument,** New Mexico

357.   11/02/90   **Weir Farm National Historic Site,** Connecticut

358.   05/24/91   **Niobrara National Scenic River,** Neb.-SD

359.   12/11/92   **Mary McLeod Bethune Council House National Historic Site,** Washington, D.C.

360.   02/24/92   **Salt River Bay National Historic Park & Ecological Preserve,** Virgin Islands.

361.   03/03/92   **Manzanar National Historic Site,** California

362.   08/26/92   **Marsh-Billings National Historic Park,** Vermont

363.   10/07/92   **Ebey's Landing National Historical Reserve,** Washington. Changed from affiliated area by NPS director.

364.   10/16/92   **Dayton Aviation National Historic Park,** Ohio

365.   10/21/92   **Little River Canyon National Preserve,** Alabama

366.   10/26/92   **Brown v. Board of Education National Historic Site,** Kansas

367.   10/27/92   **Keweenaw National Historic Park,** Michigan

Index

L

M

R

S

T

U

V

W